DOLPHINS AND PORPOISES

Look for these and other books in the
Lucent Endangered Animals and Habitats Series:

Other related titles in the Lucent Overview Series:

DOLPHINS AND PORPOISES

BY STUART A. KALLEN

Endangered Animals & Habitats

LUCENT BOOKS, INC.
SAN DIEGO, CALIFORNIA

Library of Congress Cataloging-in-Publication Data

Kallen, Stuart A., 1955–
  Dolphins and porpoises / by Stuart A. Kallen.
     p. cm. — (Endangered animals & habitats)
Includes bibliographical references (p.   ).
Summary: Describes dolphins and porpoises as rulers of the sea,
threats from fishing and hunting, pollution and habitat destruction,
dolphins and porpoises in captivity, and saving the dolphins.
  ISBN 1-56006-729-2 (hardback)
  1. Dolphins—Juvenile literature. 2. Porpoises—Juvenile literature.
[1. Dolphins. 2. Porpoises. 3. Endangered species.] I. Title. II. Series.
  QL737 .C432 K36 2001
  599 .53—dc21

                                                       00-012619

Contents

INTRODUCTION   6

CHAPTER ONE   10
Rulers of the Sea

CHAPTER TWO   26
Threats from Fishing and Hunting

CHAPTER THREE   43
Pollution and Habitat Destruction

CHAPTER FOUR   59
Dolphins and Porpoises in Captivity

CHAPTER FIVE   75
Saving the Dolphins

NOTES   93
ORGANIZATIONS TO CONTACT   95
SUGGESTIONS FOR FURTHER READING   99
WORKS CONSULTED   101
INDEX   106
PICTURE CREDITS   111
ABOUT THE AUTHOR   112

Introduction

DOLPHINS ARE SOME of the most beautiful and intelligent creatures on earth. Their playful behavior and sleek, swift forms have long inspired human fascination and affection. The seventy-nine different species of dolphins, porpoises, and related whales have thrived in the world's oceans from Japan to Europe to North America. And they have inhabited the greatest rivers on earth including the Amazon in South America and the Yangtze in China.

While observing dolphin behavior in the first century A.D., Roman naturalist Pliny the Elder wrote: "Swiftest of all animals . . . is the dolphin; it is swifter than a bird and darts faster than a javelin."[1] Pliny was not alone in his appreciation and respect for dolphins. The animals are widely depicted in ancient Greek paintings, sculpture, and pottery dating back more than thirty-five hundred years. They are also frequently mentioned in ancient Greek legends, and almost every civilization has stories of shipwrecked sailors being rescued by dolphins.

In modern times, however, dolphins and porpoises are swimming in troubled waters. Since the end of World War II, technology has reshaped large-scale fishing operations. With the use of helicopters, fish-locating radar, and massive gill nets, fishing fleets can now find and catch almost every living creature in a given area of water. Not only are dolphins and porpoises caught in these nets, but the food they rely on has been reduced to dangerously low levels in some regions.

Pollution, hunting, and captivity

In addition to the threat from fishing fleets, the waterways that dolphins live in have become increasingly polluted since the beginning of the twentieth century. A devil's brew of contaminants including raw human sewage, oil, radioactive isotopes, military toxins, and pesticides have seriously affected dolphins, porpoises, and other sea creatures.

Even though dangerous chemicals can be found in the blubber of dolphins and porpoises, people continue to hunt them for their meat. Diners in Japan, Taiwan, Norway, and elsewhere consider dolphin meat a delicacy and will pay high prices—up to seventy-five dollars a pound—to obtain it. The fact that this meat often contains dangerous levels of mercury, DDT, and PCBs has had no effect on this trade.

Dolphins' appearance and intelligence have fascinated humans for centuries.

While a small percentage of people love to eat dolphins, a much larger number may be loving them to death. Since the 1960s, sea parks and aquariums all over the world have turned dolphin and porpoise shows into big business. While these parks only use a small number of animals, many of the performing dolphins are captured in the wild and survive only a short time in captivity. Ironically, this human fascination with and affection for marine mammals has affected wild dolphin populations in several regions.

Threatened species

Although many of the seventy-nine species of dolphins and porpoises remain healthy, a number of them are in severe decline. These include dusky dolphins off the coast of Peru, Dall's porpoises and striped dolphins near Japan, Hector's dolphins off New Zealand, and white dolphins near Hong Kong. River dolphins such as the boto in the Amazon and the baiji in China are near extinction.

While these species face imminent destruction if nothing is done to save them, even the healthiest populations of dolphins and porpoises are threatened by drastic changes in the ocean. This threat can be seen in the waters off southern California, home to the bottlenose and several other species of dolphin. In that region alone, since 1955, the levels of zooplankton, microscopic floating animals that compose a vital link at the base of the food chain, have declined by more than half. These tiny creatures provide food for anchovy, jack mackerel, rockfish, and other fish that, in turn, are the main food source for dolphins. Marine biologists speculate that this decline has been caused by pollution and global warming. So while bottlenoses are not immediately threatened, the damage to their environment remains severe.

Intertwined with human life

At the beginning of the twenty-first century, there are few dolphin or porpoise species that do not face some sort of threat from overfishing, pollution, or global climate change.

Researchers know very little about how these problems affect dolphins and porpoises. Studying the animals in the

open ocean is extremely difficult and many species live far out to sea, hundreds of miles from land. They spend much of their time diving to depths that humans cannot reach without a submarine. The only time they surface is for one or two seconds to take a breath.

Although they are as mysterious as the sea, dolphins deserve respect and protection from humans—just as the health of the ocean affects dolphins and porpoises, it also influences every person on the planet, no matter where they live. As cetacean expert Kenneth S. Norris states in the *National Geographic:* "Wherever . . . I went, [I] found dolphins to be potent symbols . . . that human endeavor and the health of the natural world are intertwined. The dolphin's fate has become a gauge of where the entire earth stands."[2]

Many of the performing dolphins seen at sea parks are captured in the wild and survive only a short time in captivity.

1

Rulers of the Sea

THEY SWIM IN oceans and rivers and cannot live without water, but dolphins and porpoises are not fish. Although the animals were once known as "fish with lungs,"[3] eighteenth-century scientists realized that these creatures were mammals. Like human beings and other mammals, dolphins breathe air, are warm-blooded, and nourish their young with milk produced in mammary glands.

When modern animal classification was invented in the eighteenth century, dolphins and porpoises were classified in the scientific order Cetacea that also includes certain types of whales. In general, cetaceans are divided into three orders depending on size: Whales are large, dolphins are medium, and porpoises are small.

Dolphins and porpoises are members of the suborder known as Odontoceti, or "toothed whales." In addition to having teeth, members of the Odontoceti family all breathe through a single blowhole on the top of the head.

Included in the toothed whale family are huge marine mammals such as sperm and beluga whales. The family does not, however, include great whales such as humpbacks, minke, and blue whales because they do not have teeth and possess two blowholes.

Although the terms *dolphin* and *porpoise* are often used interchangeably, the two belong to distinctly separate suborders. Dolphins have long, pointed beaks, cone-shaped teeth, and largish single fins, called dorsal fins, on their backs. Porpoises have no beak, spade-shaped teeth, and very small or absent dorsal fins.

In scientific terms the thirty-seven species of dolphin that live in the sea belong to the family Delphinidae. These animals live in cold- and warm-water oceans throughout the world and in some bays and inlets. The four species of dolphin that live in rivers belong to the Platanistidae family, while the six species of porpoise that live in the ocean are part of the Phocoenidae family.

The physical size of the dolphin or porpoise depends on the species. The smallest dolphin, the tucuxi, is a little over 5 feet long and weighs under 100 pounds. Harbor porpoises are around 6 feet 6 inches long and weigh about 165 pounds. A male Risso's dolphin can exceed 12 feet and weigh over 1,100 pounds. The killer whale, which despite its name is actually a dolphin, may grow to 32 feet and weigh 18,000 pounds.

Powerful swimmers

As mammals, dolphins are ancestors of ancient animals who once walked the earth, and also distantly related to humans and other land animals such as dogs and horses. Over the course of millions of years, however, dolphins'

Dolphins (bottom) have long, pointed beaks and large dorsal fins, while porpoises (top) have no beaks.

bodies have evolved to allow them to spend their entire lives in water. They eat, sleep, and reproduce in rivers and oceans and never need to visit dry land. As Ben Wilson writes in *Dolphins of the World:*

> Being freed of a terrestrial base they have exploited all of the great oceans, most of the seas and several great river systems across the globe. . . . In doing so, evolution had shaped dolphins . . . to look more like fish than their land-bound forbears, but their mammalian origin has given them a legacy that includes some unexpected advantages as aquatic predators.[4]

These advantages include nearly hairless, streamlined, torpedo-shaped bodies with short, strong necks that allow the cetaceans to swim at a rapid rate. The animals propel themselves through water using powerful tail fins called flukes. Their flukes are operated by massive muscles that stretch from the belly to the tail and make up more than 30 percent of the animal's weight.

As dolphins swim, they steer and stabilize themselves with flippers, frontal appendages that have an interior bone structure containing five fingers, similar to a human hand.

In addition to flukes and fins, the rubbery skin of the dolphin helps the animals glide through the water, as Wilson explains:

> Except for a few sensory bristles [of hair] around the snout, dolphins, like all of the other cetaceans, have lost all traces of hair: Genitals and nipples are tucked away inside folds in the skin which itself is smooth and taut like the surface of a boiled egg. This cuts down on the friction of flowing water and denies a foothold for barnacles and other [parasitic] organisms. Below this rubbery exterior is a layer of blubber made from fibrous tissues and oils. It acts as a heat insulator and fat store and streamlines the body by smoothing out any lumps or bumps from the ribs, vertebrae or skull. Being lighter than water, the blubber also reduces the overall density of the dolphin, giving it more . . . buoyancy.[5]

While buoyant and elastic, cetacean skin is very sensitive to the lightest touch. This sensitivity has a strong influence on dolphin behavior because they like to be gently touched. Trainers reward dolphins by petting them, and in the wild,

Dorsal Fins

The dolphin's dorsal fin helps stabilize the animal and keeps it from spinning like a top when swimming at high speeds. In *Dolphins of the World,* Ben Wilson discusses this useful appendage:

> Most dolphins . . . have a dorsal fin. It is formed from tough fibrous connective tissue and contains no bones. Situated at the top of the back, it functions like the keel on a boat and stops the animal from pirouetting [spinning] in the water. In most species, dorsal fins are . . . shaped like swept back half crescents . . . but in several spinner dolphins populations they are tilted forwards rather than back. In some small dolphins, like the Heaviside's and Commerson's, they are rounded like one of Mickey Mouse's ears. The right whale dolphins and several river dolphins have lost their dorsal fins altogether and for them pirouetting underwater must somehow be useful.

the animals often rub against one another, caress each other with their flippers, or even rub against the hard shells of tortoises.

Dolphins are also very careful in situations where their skin might be damaged. The skin scars easily, and most adult animals have nicks and notches in their skin from bumping into prey, rocks, and man-made objects. This pattern of scars that is unique to each animal helps scientists and researchers identify and study individual cetaceans.

Diving for dinner

Dolphins and porpoises are some of the fastest swimmers in the sea. Bottlenose dolphins can achieve speeds of up to seventeen miles per hour (mph), and spotted dolphins can reach more than twenty-nine mph. The animals can only achieve these speeds in short bursts and do so by leaping out of the water in graceful arcs, picking up speed as they sail through the air. This activity is known as "running."

Dolphins and porpoises achieve speed by leaping out of the water in an activity known as "running."

Cetaceans need great supplies of food energy to swim fast and maintain a body temperature of about ninety-eight degrees Fahrenheit in cold water. This energy is provided, depending on the species, by fish such as herring, mackerel, and sardines along with ocean creatures such as shrimp, mollusks, and squid. In fact, cetaceans need large amounts of food to survive and eat up to 5 percent of their body weight every day. An average 220-pound bottlenose dolphin eats an estimated 11 pounds of food daily. With bodies requiring so much nourishment, cetaceans have adapted several unique characteristics to help them hunt and catch food.

Dolphins and porpoises are excellent divers and only need to surface every seven to ten minutes. The animals can do this because they use their lungs very efficiently. While humans, on average, only use about 30 percent of their lung capacity when taking a breath, dolphins use 80 to 90 percent. In *Dolphins,* world renowned marine researcher Jacques-Yves Cousteau describes the breathing patterns of dolphins:

> When a dolphin is not disturbed, and is swimming in a normal manner near the surface, he breathes once or twice per minute. But when he is disturbed, excited, or frightened, the rhythm increases considerably and reaches a rate of five or six times per minute.
>
> Before a deep dive, which may last seven minutes and probably longer, the dolphin hyperventilates his lungs by a series of deep, rapid breaths. This procedure increases the oxygen content of the lungs and facilitates the elimination of carbon dioxide.
>
> Unlike man, a dolphin empties and then refills his lungs almost totally with each breath, even when swimming normally.[6]

After filling its lungs with oxygen, a bottlenose dolphin can dive up to 1,750 feet below the surface. (Humans in scuba suits generally dive to a depth of only about 130 feet because of intense water pressure.) This diving capability makes the dolphin a formidable hunter able to seek out prey such as swordfish and sharks in the lower depths of the ocean.

When diving, a special plug-like muscle closes tightly around the dolphin's blowhole. When they swim to the surface to take a breath, the animals exhale an explosive burst just before reaching the surface, shooting a geyser of water vapor into the sky. A bottlenose dolphin may shoot these spurts three feet above the waves while the geysers of a sperm whale can attain heights of twenty-six feet. Wilson explains the breathing sequence:

> In calm seas, dolphins surface with their body arched like a bridge. The beak is pushed through the water surface and they exhale as their body rolls forward. When the head begins to

point back down, they inhale as the tail nears the surface. This tumbling brush with the atmosphere is silky smooth and leaves barely a ripple.[7]

Natural sonar

The ability to swim fast and dive deep makes dolphins and porpoises formidable hunters. The animals have other advantages in the water such as their large brown eyes located at the widest point of the head. These keen eyes can see above or just below the surface and rotate in a 180-degree arc. This allows the animal to see straight ahead, up and down, and even partially behind.

The dolphin's excellent vision becomes less useful as the animal dives deep below the surface. Oceans are clouded with sand, plankton, and many types of debris. At a depth of 33 feet, surface light is reduced by 80 percent and it is as dark as twilight. At 650 feet, there is total darkness. Except when surfacing to take a breath, river dolphins constantly live in darkness because rivers such as the Amazon are extremely muddy.

Cetaceans have adapted to this problem in a remarkable way, using a natural sonar system called echolocation. By sending out a series of high-pitched clicks, dolphins can determine the location of an underwater object by judging how long the sound takes to echo off the object and return to the animal.

Sound travels four and a half times faster through water than through air. When using echolocation, dolphins and porpoises generate the extremely loud clicks within their nasal sacs. These sounds are focused by the rounded forehead, called a melon, into a narrow beam that is projected in front of the animal. When the clicks bounce off an object, the echo reflects back to the dolphin's lower jaw, which transmits the sound waves to an inner ear and then to the brain. When the echo is received, the dolphin immediately transmits another click and judges the amount of time between the click and the echo. The animal's brain can interpret this split-second difference to judge its distance from an object. The different strength of the signal to each side of the

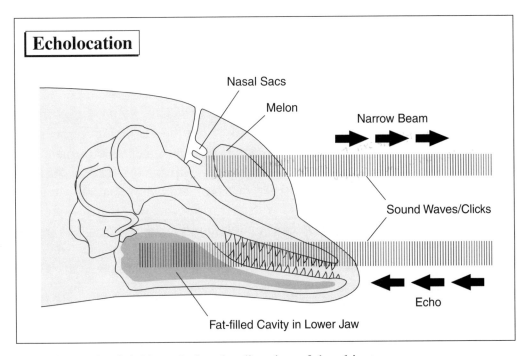

Echolocation

Nasal Sacs

Melon

Narrow Beam

Sound Waves/Clicks

Echo

Fat-filled Cavity in Lower Jaw

head allows the dolphin to judge the direction of the object, whether straight ahead or off to one side.

The organs used for echolocation also give the dolphin its gentle grin. According to the 1992 *National Geographic* article "Dolphins in Crisis" by researcher Kenneth S. Norris:

> Virtually all dolphins and porpoises share a benign "smile." It was in the 1950s that [I] determined the function behind the animals' grin: The lower jawbone flares outward and serves as an ultra-sensitive ear that enables them to hear sounds from fellow dolphins. Those sounds, emitted through the animals' . . . melons, can be heard more than a mile away by other dolphins.[8]

The cetacean sonar system is incredibly sensitive. Experiments have shown that blindfolded dolphins can swim between strings hung in the water by using echolocation. The animals also use their clicks to communicate with one another. Individual bottlenose dolphins, for example, each develop their own unique clicking whistles that help them identify each other when separated in the water.

These clicks can also express moods such as alarm, playfulness, or distress. According to Wilson: "If you are in a drifting boat near a school of dolphins and drop a hydrophone (underwater microphone) into the water you will be hit by a barrage of noise. Dolphins click, bark, yelp, bray, pop, whistle, mew and squeal."[9]

Cooperative fish gathering

Dolphins and porpoises use their complex communication systems to maintain ties with members of their own species while traveling in groups called schools or pods. Not only are these marine mammals social animals that prefer to travel with their own kind, but there is safety in numbers. Schools of dolphins are rarely attacked by predators such as sharks, but if an animal is somehow wounded, others in the pod will try to help it. Cousteau describes the situation:

> [We] have noticed that when a dolphin was injured, two or three other dolphins of the school approached to help him and support him. Meanwhile, the entire group came to a halt a short distance away, as though waiting to see what would happen. If, at the end of a certain time, the "relatives" or "friends" were not successful in getting the injured dolphin to rejoin the school, the school simply continued on its way. Those who had gone back to assist the unfortunate animal were obliged to swim after the school, for a dolphin cannot survive alone in the sea, away from others of its own kind.[10]

Such pods can number anywhere from several dozen animals to several thousand depending on the species and where they live. Spotted dolphins that live in the deep ocean, for instance, may be found in pods of more than one thousand animals. Bottlenose dolphins that live near coastal regions may travel in groups of twenty or less. Shallow-water harbor porpoises often school in groups of two to ten, while some species of river dolphin live alone.

Dolphins also use their numbers as an advantage when fishing. Most cetaceans live on fish and squid that travel in schools large enough to feed an entire pod of dolphins. If there are no fish in an area, however, dolphins can spread out across a larger region and signal to one another if they find a school of fish.

Controversial Navy Sonar Plan

Because they use echolocation to detect fish and other objects below the surface, dolphins and porpoises are extremely sensitive to loud noises in the water. In the late 1990s, the U.S. Navy began to test a new sonar method to detect enemy submarines that generated noises significantly louder than cetaceans can withstand. The navy plans to use the sonar in 80 percent of the world's oceans. The article "Navy Sonar System Threatens Marine Animals," posted on the National Resources Defense Council website (www.nrdc.org), explores this issue:

> The U.S. Navy is moving ahead with plans to deploy a new extended-range submarine detection system that will introduce into the world's oceans noise billions of times louder than that known to disturb whales [and dolphins]. This risky technology—Low Frequency Active Sonar, or LFA—represents a potentially devastating and wide-ranging threat to our planet's marine life.

> Undeniable evidence that these high-power sonar systems can and do kill marine animals emerged earlier this year, when four different species of whales and dolphins suddenly began stranding themselves across a series of islands in the Bahamas. Despite efforts to save them, seven of the creatures died. An investigative report . . . has established with virtual certainty that the mass mortality was caused by a Navy battle group using active sonar in the vicinity. . . . All but one of the whales suffered hemorrhages in the inner ear, the likely result of a sonic blast. . . .

> The Navy's new sonar is designed to detect submarines over an extended range of ocean by bombarding them with extremely intense, low-frequency sound waves. . . .

> Concern over the adverse impacts of ocean noise has risen substantially within the scientific community over the last ten years. Sound has been shown to divert [whales and dolphins] from their migration paths . . . and to induce a range of other effects from agonistic behavior to panic. A mass stranding of beaked whales off the west coast of Greece in 1996 has been associated with an LFA-type system being tested by NATO.

Once food is located, cetaceans hunt cooperatively. Pods of dolphins can round up schools of fish like cowboys herd cattle. Groups of dusky dolphins, for instance, herd large schools of anchovies into a tight ball. The fish are pushed to the surface so they cannot escape and the dolphins take turns passing through the fish ball to feed. Other species drive the fish into shallow waters where they are easily eaten.

The Greenpeace Book of Dolphins examines some instances of this communal hunting behavior:

> Two divers reported watching small groups of rough-toothed dolphins off Hawaii eat large . . . mahi-mahi [fish]. In each case, one member of the group appeared to be the keeper of the fish. Its companions swam close alongside and bit off chunks, again taking turns and showing no signs of a "feeding frenzy."[11]

Researchers believe that dolphins feed this way because they have no simple way of grasping prey. Although they can grab them in their teeth, fish are fast and agile. When they are herded together, they cannot escape and so make easier targets.

Dolphins also emit loud clicks and whistles to shock and confuse fish, making them easier to catch. Some cetaceans also use these noises to lure prey. Killer whales, for instance, emit a high-frequency sound that attracts herring, the whales' preferred food.

Community groups

While living and hunting together, cetaceans maintain interactive relationships with as many as several hundred individuals within a pod. Single male dolphins may travel with several partners that act like friends who watch out for one another. Dolphins that are related also swim together in groups consisting of a mother, brothers, and sisters.

Mothers and babies, called calves, form an especially tight bond in the pod. Dolphin calves are fully formed and almost half as large as their mothers at the moment of birth. Big babies pose problems, however. Although they are large, they are slow, making them easy prey for sharks.

Mother and calf remain close at all times, with the baby swimming beside its mother's dorsal fin. In this position, the shape and color of the animals blend together, helping hide the calf from predators. The baby can also "ride" in the slipstream—the current produced by the mother's swimming.

Calves nurse from ten to fourteen months and need large amounts of mother's milk, which is very rich and contains ten times the fat and protein as that of land mammals. When it is time to feed, the calf suckles on the mother's mammary gland that slides out through a special opening in the body. Since their mothers can never stop moving, calves must nurse while swimming, and since the baby needs to surface for air more often than its mother, the calf can nurse only for short periods of time.

Dolphins and porpoises travel together in schools, or pods, that can number anywhere from several dozen to several thousand animals.

Nursing mothers with calves rely on community cooperation when diving for food. As the mother plunges into the inky depths the calf is left floundering alone. At this time, however, nearby females will tend to the baby until the mother returns. If the calf has older brothers or sisters, they may take over the task of babysitting. If a calf's mother is killed somehow, the baby will be adopted by another female who will spontaneously produce milk, although she may not have been recently pregnant.

Even with a caring pod of mothers, brothers, and sisters, survival is difficult for calves. The two most dangerous times for young cetaceans are when they are first born and when they first separate from their mothers and must face the task of feeding themselves. Dolphins and porpoises that do survive, however, might live for fifty years or more.

Dolphin intelligence

The behavior dolphins exhibit in community groups, along with their methods of communication and use of echolocation, have led many researchers to believe that dolphins are highly intelligent creatures. Trainers and researchers who work closely with the animals note their cleverness, ability to produce complex sounds, and their playful manner—all considered signs of intelligence.

There also seems to be a strong bond between dolphins and humans. There are dozens of stories of dolphins rescuing drowning swimmers or divers in distress. Dolphins have also been known to risk their lives to fight off sharks that circled near swimmers.

Despite these factors, it is difficult for humans to measure and quantify the intellectual abilities of any creature. Cetaceans do have very large brains, and this is considered a sign of intelligence. The brain of the sperm whale, for example, is the largest of any animal, weighing about 20 pounds. This is roughly six times larger than an adult human brain, which weighs about 3.2 pounds. The brain of a bottlenose dolphin is slightly larger than that of a human, weighing 3.3 pounds.

A diver swims with a group of dolphins. A strong bond seems to exist between humans and dolphins.

Brain size alone, however, is not necessarily a measure of intellect. Researchers use the size of the brain in ratio to body size to determine brain power. For instance, the human brain is about 1.9 percent of the body weight while a bottlenose dolphin's is about half that ratio, or 0.95 percent. By comparison, a horse's brain only measures 0.15 percent of its body weight.

Since the brain is used for both thinking and controlling bodily functions such as breathing and movement, some researchers speculate that the large brain of the cetacean is necessary for the animals to sleep while swimming. Dolphins do not sleep like humans, but rather swim continuously while "napping." To do that, a dolphin closes down one half of its brain to rest while the other half keeps the animal swimming, breathing, and watching out for predators. Each half of the brain sleeps about three or four hours a day.

While marine biologists debate cetacean intellect, those who work with the animals point to obvious evidence of intelligence, as explained in *The Greenpeace Book of Dolphins:*

Talking with Dolphins

Respected biophysicist Dr. John Lilly was one of the first researchers to study dolphin intelligence and communication. His interest in the subject stimulated global interest in dolphins and motivated Congress to protect the animals with the Marine Mammal Protection Act of 1972. In his groundbreaking 1961 book *Man and Dolphin*, Lilly lists some of the humanlike noises he has heard dolphins make:

Human laughter: The explosive, repetitive, singsong ha-ha-ha! kind of laugh—the usual repetitions were in groups of three or four, with a very high-pitched child's voice quality to it. It is most distinct immediately after or within a few seconds of a woman's laughter. Repetition of human laughter may elicit further imitations either better or worse than the original.

Bronx cheers and assorted impolite (to humans) *noises:* Very raucous noises made by humans between pursed lips or between lower lip and palm can be mimicked by some young dolphins. [One particular] dolphin first showed me this set of noises and presently [another test subject] has taught it to [her calf]. Such noises are usually not encouraged in [marine parks].

Dr. John Lilly

Human words: These are the most subjective of all the judgments of the sounds emitted by dolphins. I have heard most distinctly the following words and phrases "copied" in an extremely high-pitched and brief fashion: "three-two-three," "Tee ar Pee" (the letters "TRR" were just given), and a host of others, less clear but verging so closely on humanlike rhythm, enunciation, and phonetic quality as to be eerie.

[Dolphins] live in societies marked . . . by co-operative [rather than] competitive interactions, and rapidly learn the artificial tasks given to them in captivity. Indeed, dolphins are clearly capable of learning through observation and have good memories. People who spend time with captive dolphins are invariably impressed by their sense of humour, playfulness, quick comprehension of body language, command of situations, mental agility and emotional resilience. Individual dolphins have distinctive personalities and trainers often speak of being trained by their subjects, rather than the other way around.[12]

Efficient predators

Dolphins and porpoises have evolved over 60 million years to be some of the most intelligent and efficient predators in the sea. Their basic survival, however, requires clean water, a minimum of human interference, and a large supply of fish and other prey.

Unfortunately the delicate balance of nature required for cetacean survival has been upset, and the survival of several dolphin and porpoise species hangs in the balance. Without care and protection from humans who share their habitat, it is unclear how long these strong and beautiful animals can remain the rulers of the sea.

2

Threats from Fishing and Hunting

DOLPHINS AND PORPOISES are some of the most skilled hunters of fish in the sea, and humans have used them to help locate fish for centuries. Even ancient fishermen knew that wherever pods of dolphins were circling, great schools of fish would be nearby. In centuries past, fishing fleets would accidentally catch cetaceans in their small nets and either kill the animals for food or throw them back into the water. This system caused few problems for the animals.

Since the mid–twentieth century, however, technological advances in the fishing industry have dramatically changed the ecological balance in oceans worldwide. Largely unregulated fishing fleets in recent decades have begun using several types of fishing nets and lines that have wreaked havoc on many species of cetaceans. And they continue to kill thousands of the animals every year.

When the fisheries set nets in search of squid, tuna, and other fish, they do not purposely kill dolphins and porpoises. The marine mammals, however, often become entangled in the huge nets and drown. These unfortunate creatures are known as "bycatch," unwanted animals that are later tossed overboard by fishermen.

Yellowfin tuna and dolphin destruction

The popularity of tuna, especially yellowfin tuna, has caused untold destruction to dolphin populations since the

1950s. For centuries tuna was caught with the old-fashioned, dolphin-safe, pole-and-line technique. This method was particularly effective for catching large, mature yellowfin found in the eight-million-square-mile area between Mexico and Chile known as the Eastern Tropical Pacific. The fishing fleets were aware that, for reasons unknown, yellowfin tuna are often found swimming underneath pods of dolphins.

In addition to catching more tuna, purse-seine nets have also led to the increased killing of dolphins.

In the late 1950s fishermen put aside their pole-and-line method and began using a purse seine, a new type of net that

vastly improved their catches. Purse-seine fishing utilizes a mile-long curtain-like net that can be closed off, or "pursed," at the bottom after it has surrounded thousands of tuna. Purse-seine fisheries use helicopters to spot pods of dolphins, then dispatch speedboats to circle around the dolphins and tuna to

 The Dolphin-Safe Label

When it was discovered that purse-seine tuna fishing killed millions of dolphins, consumers demanded that tuna sold in the United States not be caught with purse-seine nets. The Congressional Research Service issued this brief (available at www.cnie.org/nle/mar-14.html) that explains the confusion and controversy over "dolphin-safe" products:

[After] 1988 . . . some consumer groups began to suggest a consumer boycott of tuna caught by encircling dolphins with purse seines. In April 1990, the three largest tuna processors supplying the U.S. market responded to continuing public concerns over dolphin mortality by announcing that they would no longer purchase tuna caught in [purse-seine nets]. This action caused all but 11 of the 35 U.S. tuna seiners operating in the ETP [Eastern Tropical Pacific] to relocate to the western Pacific, where the dolphin-encirclement method of tuna fishing [could not be regulated by observers]. . . . Congress responded by enacting . . . the Dolphin Protection Consumer Information Act, to set standards for labeling tuna as "dolphin-safe.". . .

Critics of the dolphin-safe labeling policy have pointed out that these standards are misleading in that they allow tuna caught outside the ETP to be labeled as "dolphin-safe" even though the fisheries, and any dolphin mortalities, are unobserved. For example, tuna caught by gillnets in the Indian Ocean can be labeled dolphin-safe even though significant numbers of dolphins may be killed in this fishery. ETP tuna caught in purse seine nets where independent observers have verified that no dolphin mortality occurred, however, are not considered "dolphin-safe" [because purse-seine nets are used]. Thus, "dolphin-safe," as currently defined, does not mean that no dolphins are killed to catch the tuna, but that no dolphins are surrounded by purse seines in the ETP to catch the tuna.

herd them into a smaller area. Underwater explosives are thrown from the helicopters to confuse the fish—and coincidentally the dolphins—and prevent them from escaping.

After several hours of this exhausting treatment, the fish and the dolphins finally give up and form a circle for protection. The purse seine is then easily set around the creatures and hauled onto the fishing boat by a hydraulic pulley. Dolphins caught in this trap either drown or are crushed under the weight of the surrounding tuna. Flippers, fins, and beaks are torn off in the process so that even those dolphins that escape have little hope of survival.

Owners of fishing fleets, however, care little about the dolphin bycatch, because yellowfin tuna is an extremely valuable commodity. It garners a high price at the market and its large size makes it easy to process. In fact, many tuna canneries are set up to handle only yellowfin and cannot process smaller tuna species. As *The Greenpeace Book of Dolphins* states:

> Purse-seining allowed far more tuna to be caught than was possible through bait-fishing, was less labour-intensive and thus more profitable. With the realization that bountiful and financially rewarding catches awaited those willing and able to take advantage of the tuna-dolphin bond, fishery changed dramatically. The results were record catches of yellowfin and record numbers of dead dolphins.[13]

By the mid-1960s, fishermen were killing over 250,000 dolphins annually with purse-seine fishing methods. Especially hard hit were spinner dolphins, spotted dolphins, and common dolphins. An estimated 12 million spotted dolphins have been killed since 1965, and the population of spinners has been depleted by 80 percent from its pre-1950s numbers.

In 2000, eastern spinner dolphin numbers were estimated to be between one-half and one-fifth of their original abundance, while northeastern offshore spotted dolphin stocks are estimated to be about one-fifth of their original numbers. In addition over 3 million dolphins continue to be chased and harassed by purse seiners every year. No one knows if the dolphin populations in the Eastern Tropical Pacific will ever recover.

Netting nightmare

Although purse-seine nets kill dolphin species that swim with tuna, the deadliest enemy that cetaceans face is the drift gill net. Gill nets trap fish that poke their heads through the small squares of mesh in the net. When the fish try to escape, their gills become tangled in the netting. Small gill nets have been used since prehistoric times, but modern drift nets have only been in use since the early 1980s.

Drift nets are made of nonbiodegradable nylon or plastic and are up to thirty-seven miles long. They hang like curtains about sixteen feet deep in the water, prompting environmentalists to call them "walls of death." When set, the nets drift with the ocean's currents, snaring any creature that they come in contact with. The nets are equipped with radio sensors so fishing boats can follow them.

When dolphins encounter drift nets, their teeth, beaks, or fins become entangled and the animals drown. This happens to more than 1 million dolphins and porpoises of dozens of species every year. The bycatch in drift nets also includes whales, sea turtles, birds, and other wildlife. This adds up to an astounding 27 million tons of bycatch killed every year.

This fishing method has been employed across the globe. In just one region of the North Pacific over twenty thousand miles of drift nets are set every night. As Norris writes:

> Three Asian nations—Japan, Taiwan, and South Korea—have used the nets to feed their tremendous national appetites for squid and other seafood from the Pacific and Indian Oceans, while in the Atlantic several European nations have drift-netted primarily for albacore tuna. Marine mammals of the open sea, which had never before known an obstruction, had to find their way through net corridors that subdivide their world into an endless, lethal maze.

> Modern nets are made of nylon, impervious to rot and nearly as strong as steel. If sections are torn free in a storm, as frequently happens, they may continue to catch everything that encounters the mesh, even after months at sea. They become ghost nets, and nobody can count the animal life they destroy.[14]

Marine researchers estimate that over six hundred miles of this ghost netting is left in the northern Pacific each year. In fact, abandoned netting in this one region alone would stretch one-third of the way around the earth.

Drift netting is an extremely wasteful way to fish. Fishermen hunting skipjack tuna in the South Pacific, for instance, kill one dolphin or porpoise for every ten tuna caught and about 25 percent of the catch is unwanted fish species.

The cetaceans most often caught as bycatch in drift nets are Dall's porpoises, northern right whales, Pacific white-sided dolphins, and common dolphins. Japanese squid fishermen kill tens of thousands of Dall's porpoises annually. Italian fleets hunting swordfish and bonito in the Mediterranean kill about 2,000 striped dolphins every year. In the waters of New Zealand only 3,000 Hector's dolphins remain, a dangerously low number that may never recover. Between 1984 and 1988 alone, over 230 Hector's dolphins were killed in gill nets.

Pictured is a fish caught in a drift gill net. The drift gill net is perhaps the deadliest enemy cetaceans face.

Although the use of large drift nets was banned by the United Nations (UN) in 1991, nets one and a half miles long are still legal, and every day thousands of these nets are set across the world's oceans. In addition, fishing fleets ignore the UN ban and continue to use nets up to thirty miles long. Even those who use legally accepted nets continue to kill cetaceans. According to "Indiscriminate Slaughter at Sea," a National Audubon Society web page: "The number of whales and dolphins that are killed as bycatch every year in the California swordfish drift gillnet fishery is about equal to the number of all whales and dolphins in public display facilities, such as zoos and aquariums, in the entire United States."[15]

The deadly longline

When large drift nets were banned by the UN in 1991, thousands of fisheries switched to drift longlines, another fishing method that has proved to be equally destructive to cetaceans.

Longlines, used mainly in the Pacific to target swordfish and tuna, are long, single strands of untwisted synthetic nylon fiber, known as monofilament, which stretch twenty to seventy miles across the ocean. Laborers attach fifteen hundred to two thousand hooks to the longline, and each hook is baited with squid, mackerel, or some other similar fish. According to the National Audubon Society:

> Drift longlines are indiscriminate killers. Any animal large enough to bite the baited fist-sized hook is captured whether or not it is commercially valuable, juvenile or adult, targeted or unwanted. Longlines are used around the globe and primarily target high value swordfish and tuna. Each year drift longlines unintentionally kill [whales, dolphins, porpoises], threatened sea turtles, seabirds, and tens of thousands [of fish] many of which are discarded. In the Atlantic . . . fisheries for swordfish and sharks, longlines kill . . . three species of whales and dolphins.[16]

To make matters worse, around five thousand fluorescent light sticks are attached to each longline, since, for reasons unknown, these lights attract fish. The plastic light sticks often break or fall off the lines. Dolphins, porpoises, turtles, and seabirds mistakenly eat these toxic items and die.

When the damage from longlines was discovered, they were banned for use in U.S. waters by the National Marine Fisheries Service in August 2000. Their use in other parts of the world continues, however.

Hunting whales

While thousands of cetaceans die accidentally as bycatch every year, in some regions of the world large cetaceans such as gray, sperm, and right whales have been intentionally killed for food, oil, and other products for hundreds of years.

During the eighteenth and early nineteenth centuries, British, Dutch, and American whaling fleets, hunting in

During the eighteenth and nineteenth centuries, fishermen hunted whales in rowboats with hand-thrown harpoons.

rowboats with hand-thrown harpoons, virtually eliminated bowhead and northern right whales from the waters surrounding Greenland and Canada. By the 1920s English and Japanese whalers worked the southern Pacific aboard vessels known as "factory ships" upon which whales could be immediately processed into soap and margarine. These floating factories were responsible for the slaughter of more than twenty-nine thousand blue whales in 1930 alone.

Although the numbers of whales killed annually have declined in recent years, thousands of large cetaceans continue to be hunted for their valuable commercial products, as Peter G. H. Evans explains in *The Natural History of Whales and Dolphins:*

> Until recently the most important product of modern commercial whaling was oil, from baleen whales to produce margarines and other foodstuffs and from sperm whales first for lamp oil and then for specialised lubricants. However, from about 1950, meal for animal foodstuffs and chemical products became increasingly important, although baleen whale meat became even more highly valued for human consumption by the Japanese during post-war famine conditions there. The Soviet Union, the other major whaling nation in recent years, on the other hand, used very little whale meat, concentrating instead upon sperm whales for their oil. By the late 1970s, whale catches in the Antarctic were yielding 29 per cent meat, 20 per cent oil and 7 per cent meal.[17]

Today, nations such as Britain, Holland, the United States, and most others have stopped hunting whales. Only Japan and Russia continue to do so. Oil from sperm whales continues to be used in cosmetic, textile, and leather products. It is also used in pencils, crayons, and candles. Synthetic substitutes for whale oil, however, have reduced the demand for these products. And as populations of large cetaceans continue to shrink, whale oil has become very expensive both in economic and ecological terms.

Eating dolphin meat

In addition, whale meat is considered a gourmet food in Japan, and it is often sold in food markets next to dolphin

meat. And the tradition of trapping, slaughtering, and eating dolphins has a long history in that island nation. The most popular meat comes from striped dolphins, which, according to Norris, is "strong stuff—dark mahogany slabs of meat bounded by a rind of pungent blubber."[18]

Today Japan is the world's largest consumer of dolphin meat. In the past decade, dolphin meat has been promoted as an expensive delicacy to upscale urban diners in Tokyo and other large cities, selling in supermarkets for more than sixty dollars a pound.

Ironically, the meat is a human health threat since dolphins live in polluted waters and their bodies often contain high levels of mercury and other poisonous substances. Some of

Two Japanese men are shown eating dolphin meat. In Japan, dolphin meat is considered a delicacy.

Wrongly Blaming Dolphins as Competition

In many regions of the world where people rely on the fishing industry to survive, dolphins are wrongly seen as a threat to the livelihood of fishermen. This sometimes leads to tragic results for the dolphins, as detailed in *The Greenpeace Book of Dolphins:*

The battle between dolphins and the fishermen of Katsumoto on Iki Island [in] the south of Japan dates back to the early part of the twentieth century. It was then that dolphins were first blamed for disturbing the breeding grounds of the yellowtail, the Islanders' main fish catch. The killing of dolphins in the area remained sporadic, however, until 1976, when yellowtail catches declined dramatically and the fishermen protested that was because of the increased population of dolphins in the area.

This contention was widely disputed . . . because only one of the four species of dolphins that fishermen held responsible, the false killer whale, eats yellowtail and even then only as a relatively small component of its diet.

Many scientists argued that the decline was more likely to be the result of . . . large net fisheries in the area . . . [and] pollution off the coast. . . .

Nonetheless, the fishermen remained convinced that the dolphins were responsible and . . . began driving large numbers of the dolphins into bays and killing them.

Between 1976 and 1982, the Iki Islanders killed at least 4,147 bottlenose dolphins, 953 false killer whales, 525 Risso's dolphins and 466 Pacific white-sided dolphins. . . .

In 1977, the fishermen even invited television cameras to film them killing the dolphins, believing that this coverage would generate sympathy for their plight. Instead, scenes of the carnage attracted attention and condemnation from all over the world. This came as a great shock to the Iki Islanders who genuinely couldn't understand why their actions should be considered so controversial.

Feeling that dolphins were a threat to the fishing industry, Iki Islanders drove thousands into bays and killed them.

the deadliest chemicals found in the meat are polychlorinated biphenyls (PCBs), highly toxic industrial substances used to make electrical capacitors and known to cause cancer. Despite the risk, dolphin meat remains popular throughout Japan.

To satisfy the demand, dolphin hunting has long been a thriving business in the Japanese fishing village of Futo, forty miles southwest of Tokyo. When pods of dolphins are spotted, as many as twenty-four boats motor out to the school. Fishermen bang on metal pipes with hammers, driving the frightened dolphins into the shallow harbor waters where they are killed. According to Norris, "On these days the harbor runs red with blood."[19]

The situation in Futo is repeated in at least nine nearby fishing villages and striped dolphins are only one species hunted in this manner. Spotted dolphins, bottlenose dolphins, short-finned pilot whales, and false killer whales are also killed. Other species that are impossible to herd into shallow waters, such as the Pacific white-sided dolphin and Dall's porpoise, are hunted by men in small boats who shoot them with harpoon guns.

In 1988, at least 46,273 small cetaceans were killed in Japanese coastal waters. Worse yet, of these animals nearly 40,000 were one species, Dall's porpoises, of which only about 105,000 individuals are known to exist.

Such events bring worldwide condemnation by environmental groups. In spite of tens of thousands of e-mails and letters of protest to government officials, however, the dolphin-hunting season remains an annual event every autumn even in the twenty-first century. In October 1999, the season began in the traditional home of Japanese whaling, the small port town of Taiji 280 miles southwest of Tokyo. Hunters slaughtered 2,400 dolphins, porpoises, and small whales during the season that ended at the beginning of May 2000. And Taiji is only one town that participates in the centuries-old tradition. With the participation of several other port towns, more than 17,000 dolphins are killed every year.

Dolphins are not only taken for food in the region. In October 1999, 70 bottlenose dolphins were herded into Futo Bay. According to The Dolphin Link website:

> [The dolphin hunters] were met by representatives of two Japanese oceanaria (marine theme parks) who had offered . . . $30,000 per dolphin for use in their dolphin shows. The theme park representatives selected six young, unblemished dolphins, separated them from their families, put them in slings and trucked them away.
>
> The remainder of the dolphins were hauled, still living, from the water and dumped into trucks, carted to a nearby dock and butchered. . . .
>
> The incentive to the fishermen for hunting and killing the dolphins comes from the large sums of money offered for dolphins destined for captivity. In this case approximately $180,000 was on the table if the fishermen brought in six suitable bottlenose dolphins.[20]

Cetacean slaughter

Japan is only one country that kills cetaceans as part of a cultural tradition. The situation is similar in the Faeroes, a cluster of about thirty islands halfway between Scotland and Iceland. The islands were settled by Norwegians in the ninth century, but today they are a protectorate of Denmark. The forty-six thousand people who live on the islands are completely dependent upon fishing for their livelihoods. The hunting of long-finned pilot whales, a species of dolphin, has been a tradition there for more than four hundred years.

Pilot whales are twelve to nineteen feet in length and weigh up to seven thousand pounds. They often swim close to the Faeroes in the summer. When the animals are spotted by local fishermen, a hunt known as the *grindadrap*, or grind, commences.

Fishing boats form a semicircle around the whales and drive them toward the coast. Captains call ahead to alert people on the shore who wade out into the water and bury five-pound hooks called gaffs into the heads of the animals. The gaffs are attached to ropes and the whales are

Villagers butcher whale meat along the coast during the traditional whale hunt in the Faeroes.

hauled ashore where they are killed. The water runs red with blood as the animals are butchered. When the hunt is over, the meat and blubber are distributed free of charge to the inhabitants of the island.

Throughout the 1970s an average of about 1,000 pilot whales were killed each year. In the 1980s that number doubled to 2,000 or more. In addition, in one year, 1988,

544 Atlantic white-sided dolphins were killed in only one day. The killing and eating of so many cetaceans has disturbing implications, according to *The Greenpeace Book of Dolphins:*

> Of particular concern is the fact that the whales are taken from a population whose size has not been assessed. The scientists do not even know whether there are one, two, or more large pilot whale stocks in the North Atlantic. Nor is there any certainty about whether or not the whales are being affected by other human activities such as pollution, entanglement in nets or over-fishing.
>
> Ironically, there's a great deal of evidence to suggest that pilot whale meat is hazardous to the islanders' health. Pilot whales in the North Atlantic, along with many other species of marine mammals, are heavily contaminated with mercury.[21]

In spite of continued international protests, pilot-whale hunting continues in the twenty-first century.

Sea pig, crab bait, and chicken feed

While people in wealthy societies such as the Faeroes hunt whales for sport, the animals are also hunted by people who depend on cetacean meat for their very survival. Native tribes in places such as Greenland, the Arctic, and the Solomon Islands in the Pacific, for example, hunt endangered narwhal, beluga whale, and harbor porpoise to feed their families. Dolphins killed by subsistence hunters are required by law to be used only for food, oil, or other traditional uses and cannot legally be sold. There is little regulation over this practice, however, and some hunters have found it difficult to resist large sums of money paid for dolphin meat.

Dolphin hunting has also become a thriving commercial business in South America since the mid-1970s. When fish stocks were depleted as a result of overfishing along the coast of Peru, local fishermen switched to catching dusky, rough-toothed, common, and bottlenose dolphins and Burmeister's porpoises as a way to earn a living. The animals are often brought to port alive and suffocated with plastic bags forced into their blowholes. The meat is referred to as *muchame*, or "sea pig."

The Norwegian Whale Hunt

Like the Faeroe Islands hunt, the traditional annual Norwegian minke whale hunt has generated ongoing protests over the years. Every year an average of 250 minkes, which are related to dolphins but can weigh up to twenty thousand pounds, are killed by Norway's whalers. In 1998 that number increased to 624. Between 1987 and 1993, international protests and a ban by the International Whaling Commission stopped the hunt. But Norway stubbornly resumed killing minkes in the face of these objections.

Greenpeace protesters attempting to interfere with the hunt have been threatened by knife-wielding whalers and shot at with harpoons and rifles. Protesters have had a difficult time halting the hunt because of the huge profits that can be made by whalers. Each whale is worth about $10,000 to fishermen, and even more to processors who sell the meat in Norway and Japan for more than $130 a pound.

The Peruvian government outlawed fishing, killing, or processing dolphins in 1990. Peru's people, however, are very poor and little is done to stop the common practice of selling dolphin meat door-to-door.

While dolphin meat may feed hungry people in Peru, the king crab industry in Chile often uses the butchered meat of the black dolphin—one of the world's most endangered cetaceans—to provide bait in crab pots. In 1998, over two thousand rare black dolphins were used for this purpose. Around the globe in Turkey, about forty thousand endangered Black Sea dolphins are killed every year to produce chicken feed.

The controversy continues

The hunting of dolphins, porpoises, and whales is controversial whenever and wherever it happens. In recent decades, graphic video images of seas flowing with dolphin blood and butchered porpoise carcasses littering docks have elicited dispute across the globe. To those who hunt cetaceans as part of centuries-old tradition the protests mean little. Enough people are convinced, however, that dolphins and porpoises are crucial elements in the ecology of the world's oceans. People on both sides debate the issues while marine mammals are caught in the middle.

3

Pollution and Habitat Destruction

THERE IS LITTLE doubt that hunting and fishing pose a great danger to the ongoing survival of many dolphin and porpoise species. These actions, however, can be slowed or stopped when necessary with public condemnation and new laws.

There is another, more serious threat to cetaceans, and indeed all aquatic creatures, that is much harder to halt in the modern industrialized world. Since the early part of the twentieth century, porpoises and dolphins have faced an ever-increasing number of toxic chemicals that have been carelessly dumped in rivers, lakes, and oceans. These chemicals include pesticides such as chlordane and DDT; heavy metals such as mercury and cadmium used in industry; oil from wells and tankers; and raw sewage with waste from humans and farm animals. In addition rivers and oceans are filling with plastics and other garbage that have deadly consequences for marine mammals.

Unlike fishing and hunting, which are easier to regulate, pollution comes from millions of sources. This widespread problem has no easy answers, as *The Greenpeace Book of Dolphins* states:

> It is now widely recognized by governments, scientists and the general public that we are polluting the world on an unprecedented scale. The fragile net of interconnections that makes up the planet's living fabric is being disrupted by our actions: by patterns of exploitation and recreation, by flows of wastes and effluents, by thoughtlessness and greed.

Many dolphin populations are now subject to a cocktail of pollutants, a confluence of human pressures and a conflict of interest. . . . The current plight of the dolphins and other marine mammals is the first indicator of wider problems in the marine environment. It may also be symptomatic of a deep-seated disharmony between human development and the natural world.[22]

Ganges River susu

Few marine mammals are exposed to as much industrial pollution, raw sewage, and garbage as freshwater river dolphins, which are forced to live in close proximity to modern civilization.

One such animal is the Ganges River dolphin or susu, found in India, Nepal, Bangladesh, and elsewhere. The susu is black in color, five to eight feet long, and virtually blind although it can detect darkness and light. The susu swims on its side using long clicks of echolocation to find shrimp and fish while sweeping its long snout through the murky waters to grab prey.

At one time there were hundreds of thousands of these animals swimming in the Ganges River system and its tributaries. Today there are fewer than four thousand susu, with less than forty in Nepal.

The susu is threatened on all sides. It is hunted for its meat and fur and its blubber is used to fuel oil lamps. The animal also drowns in the profusion of gill nets that are found in the river. And every year more than 6 million tons of pesticides are used along the banks of the Ganges. These chemicals, which are related to nerve gas used in war, do not break down in the soil and are washed into rivers when it rains.

Bernd Würsig of Texas A&M's marine mammal program explained how toxic chemicals harm dolphins:

Dolphins . . . wear a coat of blubber, a fat layer that protects them from cold. . . . But the blubber also serves as a depot for food. Usually when a dolphin swallows a toxic pollutant, its body somehow steers the dangerous molecules into the fat layer where they simply accumulate and temporarily do no harm. . . . [Everything] is fine until the dolphin is put under stress for some reason and has to call on this food store.

45

Deadly Effects of Pollution

A Field Guide to Whales and Dolphins in the Philippines by Jose Ma. Lorenzo Tan spells out the deadly problems pollution causes in cetaceans:

Our coastal seas are becoming more and more noxious each year from the unchecked flows of industrial wastes, urban wastes and agricultural run-offs. These heavy concentrations of toxic chemicals and metals find their way into the marine life that live off these coastal areas. Toxins in the water are absorbed by small organisms, then distilled. Fish that eat these small organisms absorb these toxins and concentrate them further. With each step in the food chain, the contaminants grow to larger and larger doses. [Cetaceans] are top predators in aquatic food chains all over the world. They ingest . . . fish [and] squid . . . each day along with a high concentration of toxins earlier ingested by their prey. Some poisons are expelled through [their] normal excretions. However, amounts of toxins undoubtedly remain in their blubber, their liver, kidneys and brain. PCBs and other poisons, it has been found, are stored in fat. Mother's milk, being a fat, is the vehicle through which these toxic substances are transferred from mother to calf. Young [dolphins and porpoises], therefore, are now poisoned from the first time they nurse. . . . Whale and dolphin meat, therefore, potentially contain higher concentrations of PCBs and other toxic substances than any other animals of the sea. In one case in the St. Lawrence Estuary off Quebec, [Canada,] 88 carcasses of beluga whales washed ashore over a 5 year period. They were found with horrible diseases never seen before in whales including cancer, hepatitis, blood infections, lesions, ruptures of pulmonary arteries, ten times the previous number of tumors, perforated ulcers and indications of immuno-suppression disease [resembling AIDS]. One whale was found with PCBs, myrex, benzoate pyrines, chlorodine, a variety of insecticides, mercury and other heavy metals. The dead whales were so contaminated that, technically, they should have been considered toxic wastes.

Dead beluga whales that washed ashore in Canada were found to have horrible diseases.

If that happens, and it may happen for any of 10,000 reasons, the dolphins can die quickly, as the harmful molecules flood back into its system in a rush. These pollutants include some of the most violent poisons known, and many of them disrupt normal physiological processes.[23]

Factories and dams

Dams and factories along the Ganges and Indus Rivers threaten the susu and Indus River dolphin population.

The Ganges is lined with factories such as sugar mills, distilleries, paper mills, and chemical plants that discharge millions of gallons of pollution into the water every year. In addition, about 50 percent of India's population—10 percent of the world's population—lives along the Ganges.

The raw sewage from about seven hundred towns and cities washes into the river daily.

Besides being threatened by pollution, the susu has lost most of its habitat. Hundreds of dams for electrical and irrigation purposes have been built along the Ganges River system in the past century. These dams create artificial lakes behind them that destroy the susus' natural river environment.

In Pakistan, dams also threaten the Indus River dolphin, a close cousin to the susu. There are so many concrete dams across the Indus that the dolphin population has been segmented and divided, making it impossible for the animals to find breeding partners.

In 1974, the Pakistani government established the Indus Dolphin Reserve along a one-hundred-mile stretch of the river. Despite this protection, susus continue to suffer the effects of water pollution even in their sanctuary. According to an article by Nadeem Iqbal on the Eco web page:

> Scientific studies of the Indus water between the Guddu and Sukkur [dams], which was declared a dolphin sanctuary in the early 1970s, has confirmed the presence of heavy metals like copper, mercury and manganese.
>
> Experts say that these metals can seriously affect the normal functioning of the dolphin's reproductive system and even make it infertile. This stretch of the Indus is polluted by urban sewage from Sukkur city and a thermal power plant at Guddu.
>
> According to senior Pakistani wildlife official Umeed Khalid, river pollution is threatening the growth of numbers of the Indus dolphin.[24]

This breeding problem has alarmed researchers since there are only five hundred Indus River dolphins alive. With a swiftly plummeting population count, the susu is one of the rarest mammals in the world and one of the most threatened of all dolphin species.

The pink dolphin

The susu and Indus River dolphins struggle to survive in densely populated regions that have been developed for centuries. But the Amazon River dolphin, also known as the pink dolphin or boto, has found its habitat severely disrupted only in the past few decades.

 Threats to the Yangtze River Dolphin

The Yangtze River dolphin is one of the most endangered marine mammals on the planet, as reported in a December 5, 1997, article by Rone Tempest in the *Los Angeles Times:*

> [The] large, freshwater, whitefin dolphin—known . . . as the "baiji" dolphin . . . [or] Yangtze River dolphin is dying off at an alarming rate. Biologists believe that fewer than 100 of the rare dolphins remain in the lower reaches of the great Chinese river, the only place on Earth where the 300- to 500-pound aquatic mammals with long, beaklike snouts are found.
>
> Their survival is so uncertain that when Wang Ding, the director of the river dolphin program at China's Institute of Hydrobiology here, went out with 500 searchers in early November to conduct the annual census, he was afraid he would find none at all.
>
> On the first day out, the searchers, surveying the river on tiny 4.5-horsepower fishing boats, spotted six of the dolphins. After a week, they counted 21. Thousands once frolicked in China's most famous river, inspiring the country's greatest poets to create myths and legends about river goddesses and mermaids. . . .
>
> The Yangtze River dolphin is the rarest of all cetaceans. . . . Their habitat is in one of the world's busiest and most industrialized rivers.
>
> The dolphins are threatened by fishermen, who snag the mammals with their nets and giant hooks, and by the propeller screws of oceangoing ships that ply the lower reaches of the Yangtze. The acute sonar hearing of the practically blind dolphins is thrown off by the noise of the river traffic.
>
> A new threat to their survival was posed when workers completed the first phase of the massive Three Gorges Dam, effectively blocking the dolphins' path to the upper Yangtze.

The boto is the largest river dolphin, with a blue-gray or bright pink body that grows up to eight feet in length and weighs up to 350 pounds. The animals live on fish, crabs, and turtles in the slow-moving, muddy waters of the Amazon and Orinoco Rivers, which run through the tropical rain forests of South America. When the rivers overflow their banks during the flood season between December and June, the boto swim into the flooded forests and grasslands surrounding the river.

Since the 1970s the Amazon River basin has been undergoing rapid development. Thousands of square miles of rain

The boto is the world's largest river dolphin, weighing up to 350 pounds.

forest have been clear-cut with some of the trees being manu-factured into paper at mills that have severely polluted the rivers. One paper mill alone, located on the Jari River, dis-charges 5.2 million tons of pollution into the water every year. The effluent contains chlorine, magnesium, aluminum, and other chemicals that are toxic to the boto and the fish that it feeds on.

The Amazon is also rich in gold, and a modern-day gold rush has caused severe pollution in the region. In Brazil, miners have released thousands of tons of mercury into the water after it was used to purify gold nuggets.

The boto's river habitat is being severely threatened not only by pollution but also by the Brazilian government, which has plans to build more than sixty hydroelectric dams in the Amazon basin by 2010. While this ambitious plan is far behind schedule, seven have already been built. These dams wipe out fish species and act as barriers that separate the boto from their food sources. *The Greenpeace Book of Dolphins* explains:

> The damming of one river in the State of Pará in Brazil led to the loss of 17 out of the 22 fish species found there; only two of the remaining five [species] left are still abundant. The botos' general feeding patterns include 50 species of fish; having their diet reduced to only two species might prove fatal.[25]

Fishermen also kill botos because they are seen as compe-tition for fish. One of the most bizarre reasons dolphins are killed anywhere, however, concerns the peculiar belief that the male boto can transform itself into human form and se-duce unsuspecting women. This superstitious belief is used to explain unwanted pregnancies and has also given the dol-phin a reputation for increasing sexual potency in men. As a result, the dried eyes and sexual organs of the boto are sold as aphrodisiacs in markets throughout the Amazon region.

Plastic pollution

Although river dolphins face the greatest dangers from pollution and habitat destruction, rivers are also used as garbage dumps for household and industrial waste. Every-thing from used motor oil to food scraps and cleaning prod-ucts gets thrown into rivers that flow through urban areas.

The most common trash—and the most menacing—is the plastic junk that people throw out every day. And since all rivers eventually run to the sea the oceans are increasingly filling up with this floating garbage. According to Norris:

> The open oceans still seem quite clean, but severe pollution threatens many coastlines and bays, especially in the Mediterranean, Black, North, and Baltic Seas. Agricultural runoff and industrial waste have introduced toxic chemicals, and the [by-products] of civilization—fragments of fishing gear, polystyrene cups, plastic bags, and kitchen trash from ships' galleys—are found everywhere, on the distant beaches of Tierra del Fuego and the Aleutian Islands as well as in the harbors of Miami and Marseille.[26]

Plastic pollution is an insidious threat to dolphins and other marine mammals.

The plastics mentioned by Norris are an insidious problem because dolphins and other marine mammals often mistake plastic bags for jellyfish, one of their favorite foods. When the bags are eaten, they lodge in the animal's intestinal tract and cause a painful, lingering death.

Like plastic bags, helium balloons are extremely hazardous to marine mammals. Although they are often released on or near shore, balloons can blow over two hundred miles out to sea, often in large clusters. Once deflated they are transported on ocean currents to areas where dolphins live in the open sea. Dolphins often eat these balloons and soon die from the effects.

An example of this problem was seen in 1993, when a group of veterinarians responded to the stranding of a whale in New Jersey. The emaciated animal was taken to an aqua park and the veterinarians tried unsuccessfully for several months to feed it.

The whale continued to lose weight and was on the verge of death when doctors inserted a tiny camera into its gastrointestinal tract. The medical staff discovered that the whale had several pieces of plastic in its intestines, including an entire Mylar party balloon, the cellophane from a box of cigarettes, and pieces of a garbage bag. The plastic was successfully removed during a series of five operations. After six months, the healthy whale was released in waters off Florida. While this story had a happy ending, an untold number of dolphins, porpoises, and other sea creatures continue to die from plastic ingestion every year.

Dolphin die-offs

Researchers can occasionally determine a specific cause of death when confronted with a dead or dying cetacean. Since the 1980s, however, there has been a major increase in dolphin die-offs whose causes remain a mystery.

One of the most serious die-offs occurred in the summer of 1987 when huge numbers of sick and dying bottlenose dolphins washed up on beaches along the coast of New Jersey. Over the next six months more than 750 of the animals were found on the Atlantic coast from New Jersey to

Florida. Researchers estimate that many hundreds more died unseen and uncounted at sea, and approximately 50 percent of the entire Atlantic Coast bottlenose population died at this time.

Even more puzzling, the dolphins were horribly scarred as if they had been swimming in hydrochloric acid. Brian Gorman, the spokesperson for the National Oceanic and Atmospheric Administration (NOAA), stated, "It was like nothing in recorded history. . . . The dolphins were coming in, their skin falling off, sores and lesions all over their bodies."[27]

Harassed by Boats

Just as more automobiles are crowding the highways, an increasing number of recreational watercraft are filling America's bays, rivers, and coastal waterways. Dolphins and porpoises are run over, mangled by boat propellers, and harassed by drivers of personal watercraft. The animals have become increasingly nervous on crowded weekends when they are forced to share their habitat with recreational boaters. Kenneth S. Norris wrote in the September 1992 *National Geographic* about this problem as it affects dolphins in Sarasota Bay, Florida:

> Few speed limits restrained the long "cigarette boats" and giant motor-yacht castles—whose proprietors stood in the sterns with highball glasses in hand—that swashed by. [Our boat] rocked crazily in the double wake of one and, as the water calmed, [we] noted a cluster of gray dolphins plunging along with us.

> "What do dolphins think about all this traffic?" I asked [my guide]: "Well . . . I can tell you that after a weekend, when this channel really goes crazy [with boat traffic], the dolphins tend to be quite skittish and difficult to approach. They don't recover for a day or two. The worst are the Jet Skis, because they aren't limited to the channels. They can go anywhere."

> Two of these machines snarled by, doing crazy eights all over the shallows. I wondered how long it would be before this invasion broke the delicate balance that allowed the dolphins to regard us as benign. The shallows are the last refuge of the dolphins, whose forebears probably swam in this bay long before the first Europeans came to the New World.

Dolphins and porpoises are often run over and harassed by boats and other recreational watercraft.

Dolphins were not the only victims of this mysterious poisoning. Millions of fish also washed up on the shores of New York and New Jersey, along with an unprecedented amount of raw sewage, tar balls, and used syringes. Swimmers who went into the regional waters at this time became ill, and beaches up and down the East Coast were closed by authorities.

For the next several years marine biologists and government researchers studied the problem and offered often conflicting reasons for the die-off. NOAA issued a report in 1989 declaring that the animals had died from natural toxins known as red-tide algae. This algae is produced when a type of one-celled organism called phytoplankton periodically experiences rapid growth because ocean temperature and nutrients are favorable to such growth. These blooms are red in color and give the phenomenon its name. One type of plankton that grows during the red tide also produces a poison known as brevetoxin. Government researchers speculated that dolphins ate fish tainted with the poison, and while it did not kill them it weakened their immune systems enough so that they could not resist pollution in the water.

Conflicting opinions

Many nongovernment marine biologists doubted the red-tide theory because algae blooms had been common occurrences, and in past years they had never resulted in such massive dolphin die-offs. At the insistence of these researchers and several environmental groups, Congress held hearings to investigate the deaths.

The red-tide theory was called into question by dozens of marine mammal biologists. Several researchers testified that the government purposely overlooked the presence of industrial pollution—especially PCBs—in the dolphin bodies. Independent research showed that the PCB levels in these animals was the highest ever found in cetaceans. Government regulations require that any chemical found to have more than 5 parts per million (ppm) of PCBs be handled as toxic waste. By comparison, the beached dolphins had up to 620 ppm of the cancer-causing substance. One animal had a staggering 6,800 ppm in its blubber.

PCBs are known to cause skin lesions and liver damage, and harm nervous, reproductive, and immune systems. The area near New Jersey where the main die-off had occurred was known to be a dumping ground for sewage and acids, as well as chemical warfare agents manufactured for the military at nearby industrial plants. According to *The Greenpeace Book of Dolphins,* however:

> The U.S. government certainly appeared anxious to avoid the implication of PCBs, or any other form of pollution, in the dolphins' deaths. In a leaked memo, read out at the Congressional hearing, one government scientist asked another for "data it generated on PCB/pesticides." He added that no matter what was found in the dead dolphins, "no special attention will be drawn to [this] data. . . . [And] a blanket statement will be made that the levels were not out of the ordinary."[28]

Many causes

While the government hearings never proved conclusive, there is little doubt that the dolphin die-off was caused by a number of problems that are becoming more common. Sewage and industrial pollution cause an ever-increasing number of beaches to be closed every year, and almost every species of marine life, many of which dolphins prey on, has been affected by environmental contamination.

Worldwide water pollution is getting worse every year, and many species of dolphins live near the most heavily industrialized cities in the world. One Dutch researcher estimated that as bad as the problem is, as little as 5 percent of the PCBs stored as toxic waste have made their way into the ocean. As much as 50 percent more is expected to wash into the seas in the coming decades.

In addition, red tides are now commonly killing cetaceans around the globe where they have not had an effect in earlier years. Researchers speculate that the growing number of red tides is caused by ever-increasing levels of fertilizer and sewage washing into the ocean every year. These fertilizers feed the algae responsible for the red tides and cause them to

Some researchers speculate that the red tide is responsible for the increase in dolphin deaths.

occur with greater frequency and intensity. Some also point to global warming and the warmer temperatures in the ocean as fostering red-tide algae.

While dolphins continue to die, researchers find no easy answers. In 1997 more than 162 dolphins were found dead in the Gulf of California in Mexico. Government authorities were unable to confirm if the dolphins had died from a red-tide outbreak or from toxic chemicals thrown in the ocean by drug traffickers. During a three-month period in the autumn of 1999, about 75 dead or dying dolphins washed ashore during a red-tide outbreak in Florida along the Gulf of Mexico. While these animals were affected by the red tide, researchers believed that their immune systems were considerably weakened for reasons unknown, and that the animals were unable to resist the algae that might not have harmed them in earlier years.

Top of the food chain

Marine mammals such as dolphins and porpoises are at the top of the aquatic food chain. This means that the pollution that harms the lowest life forms in the sea also affects the fish that cetaceans need to thrive. When dolphins wash ashore with burns and lesions on their bodies it shows that something is seriously wrong with the entire web of life in the ocean environment. Human beings across the globe depend upon the oceans and rivers for a large percentage of their food, but they have also been using these same waterways as garbage dumps and for hazardous waste disposal. Biologists believe that the fate of the dolphins is a sure sign that humanity needs to change its attitudes toward rivers and oceans before it is too late.

4

Dolphins and Porpoises in Captivity

POLLUTION AND HABITAT destruction remain the biggest threats to dolphins and porpoises. Populations of these animals are also being reduced in some regions because, ironically, they are being loved to death. Every year hundreds of dolphins, porpoises, and small whales are violently captured by hunters who sell them to zoos, marine parks, aquariums, and even to hotels for display in swimming pools.

Dolphin display has become a big business. People pay millions of dollars every year to these institutions so that they can observe dolphins, see them do tricks, and even swim with them. Such displays have increased the popularity of dolphins and inspired thousands of people to help save them in their natural state. Unfortunately, the survival rates for the animals taken into captivity are not good.

Fifty-three percent of captured dolphins die within three months in their new environment. The surviving half die within their first two years of captivity. The few that survive longer live only an average of five years, compared with thirty-five years in the open ocean. And during every seven-year period, half of all dolphins in captivity die from shock, pneumonia, intestinal disease, ulcers, chlorine poisoning from the water in their tanks, or stress-related illnesses.

Not all experts agree, however, that keeping dolphins in captivity is bad. While at least forty-six hundred dolphins, porpoises, and killer whales have been captured in the past thirty years, some argue that the educational value of seeing these animals close-up overrides concerns about individual animals being forced to live in captivity. The concept of the marine park, however, is disturbing to those who claim that keeping intelligent and magnificent animals in captivity is cruel and provides little real education. As naturalist and oceanographer David Suzuki stated:

> [We] must ask what message we receive from watching captive [cetaceans]. When they perform tricks they have learned from their trainers, the animals merely reinforce the message that humankind reigns supreme of the natural world. And what do we learn about the life and behaviour of creatures that are beautifully honed by evolution to roam over vast distances and that share tight familial and social bonds, which we barely understand? The intelligence of [dolphins] is undeniable, so we must wonder what psychological and physiological trauma confinement inflicts on them.[29]

History of captivity

Some of the most intelligent creatures found in sea parks are dolphins known as orcas. These six-thousand- to eighteen-thousand-pound black-and-white animals with huge dorsal fins are also referred to as killer whales. Orcas are one of the most wide-ranging mammals on earth and easily travel between ice-cold polar regions and warm tropical waters.

In spite of their name, orcas are not killers at all, except to the fish, squid, and seals they prey upon. Instead, the behavior of killer whales is usually inquisitive and friendly toward humans approaching them in boats. It is this behavior that has made them so easy to capture.

Orcas such as Shamu the Killer Whale are a multimillion-dollar business today for oceanariums such as Sea World in California and Florida. In the early 1960s, however, researchers had no idea how such large animals would survive in captivity. And at that time, attempts at capturing these magnificent wild animals resulted in tragedy.

In 1961, one of the first large-scale oceanariums in the world, Marineland of the Pacific, near Los Angeles, sent out a crew to collect dolphins. The crew found a female orca swimming off the coast of Newport. The animal was captured and placed in a tank but attempted to escape by repeatedly swimming into the concrete walls. The next day she was dead. A year later the crew caught another orca in a net but the killer whale and a companion began ramming the boat and hitting it with their tail flukes. The panicked crew killed one animal and scared the other one away.

Orcas harassed in such a manner project loud warnings to the other animals in their pod. As author Erich Hoyt

During the 1960s, attempts to capture orcas (killer whales) often resulted in tragedy.

states, "These . . . captives were vocalising in sudden outbursts of urgent yet seemingly despondent tones. They were distress calls. They were loud. Underwater, they would carry about seven miles; on the surface, under ideal conditions, perhaps a few hundred yards."[30]

Moby Doll makes waves

In 1964 the unexpected popularity of orcas was demonstrated when the Vancouver Pacific Aquarium in British Columbia, Canada, hired a sculptor to kill an orca to use as a model for a giant sculpture. The artist harpooned a young killer whale near the coast of British Columbia but it did not die. Instead, the aquarium's director ordered the crew to tow the wounded orca back to Vancouver. After a torturous sixteen-hour journey through choppy seas, the young whale was placed in a small dockside pen.

Mistaking the male orca for a female, the crew named the animal "Moby Doll." When the press spread word about the capture of this animal, more than ten thousand people from across the globe flocked to Vancouver to see the first killer whale in captivity.

The wounded animal eventually healed but would not eat for more than seven weeks. Finally, after fifty-five days, Moby began eating more than two hundred pounds of food a day. Four weeks later, however, Moby died from unknown causes.

The managers of the Vancouver Pacific Aquarium realized that they had accidentally stumbled upon an extremely profitable idea. During Moby's short time in its makeshift pen, its keepers discovered that, contrary to legend, killer whales were quite docile and could be kept in captivity like other zoo animals. In addition, with food as an incentive, the orcas could be trained to perform tricks like circus animals. And the fearsome reputation of the killer whale, combined with its "cuddly" charm, had the ability to draw huge crowds.

These points quickly became obvious to aquarium managers outside of Vancouver. Within a year the Seattle Public

History of Captive Dolphins

Large-scale for-profit marine parks that display dolphins and small whales are a relatively new concept. *Whales, Dolphins, and Porpoises,* edited by Mark Carwardine, explores the history of cetaceans on display for the general public:

> In the 1870s, five belugas were on display to the public in England, and bottlenose dolphins and harbor porpoises were kept in the Battery Aquarium, New York, in 1913. However, the latter were not very popular due to a tendency to exhibit "overt sexual behavior.". . . In the 1930s the Aquarium of the Marine Biological Association of the United Kingdom at Plymouth periodically displayed animals rescued from live strandings, but did not begin to keep animals permanently until about 1962, when two female bottlenose dolphins were obtained.

> In 1938, Marine Studios, a Hollywood film company, set up a marine tank in Florida, primarily to shoot underwater footage of dolphins. The dolphins became a tourist attraction, and a curator was appointed to train them. This was the first prolonged observation of dolphins' social life and behavior, and signaled the beginning of the development of marine mammal facilities all over the world. . . .

> During the 1970s, the number of captive facilities increased dramatically throughout North America, Europe, Japan and parts of Southeast Asia. Many of them still exist today, and new facilities continue to swell their ranks. They include a motley collection of netted pools, concrete tanks and even hotel swimming pools. The captive animals are often trained to "kiss" their trainers, fetch balls, jump through hoops, perform somersaults and make synchronized leaps in special shows for the fee-paying public. The vast majority are put on display purely for financial profit.

Captured dolphins are trained to perform many tricks, including "kissing" their trainers.

Aquarium in Washington put a large male orca named Namu on display. The animal had been purchased from two Canadian fishermen for eight thousand dollars after they had accidentally snared the animal in their gill net. Several months later, the aquarium's owners captured Shamu, a female that they intended to mate with Namu. Although the pair did not breed, they performed tricks together for about a year until Namu died. Shamu was sold to Sea World in San Diego, which opened in 1964. Since that time the popularity of dolphins and porpoises has increased dramatically with the general public and has grown into a multimillion-dollar business.

A booming business

Shamu was captured by the owner of the Seattle Aquarium, Ted Griffin, and his assistant, Don Goldsberry. In the mid-1960s, these two men developed methods for capturing and shipping orcas that were later imitated by others.

The Griffin-Goldsberry method involves surrounding a pod of orcas with a purse-seine net. The best looking specimen is lifted from the sea with a sling which is then hung in a large wooden box cooled by blocks of ice. The box is loaded onto a transport ship, truck, or cargo plane for shipping to a specific sea park.

The docile personalities of the orcas make this job relatively easy and collectors remark that the animals could easily escape the nets if they choose to do so. The hazards to the overall orca population, however, are anything but harmless. In August 1970, Griffin and Goldsberry rounded up eighty killer whales at Penn Cove, Washington. As *The Greenpeace Book of Dolphins* states:

> Never before or since have so many whales been captured at once. Although they were unaware of it at the time, Griffin and Goldsberry had captured three pods traveling together. Those 80 whales comprise almost the entire "resident" orca population off southern Vancouver Island and in Puget Sound. For a day, until they released the majority of the whales, the fate of an entire "community" or breeding stock of orcas was in the hands of unregulated collectors.

As news of the capture spread, aquarium orders poured in. Seven whales were shipped to aquaria in Japan, England, France, Australia and the US.[31]

By the 1970s there were several teams of collectors from around the world taking advantage of the booming demand for killer whales. There were no regulations on this practice, and many animals that were not captured were wounded in the process. Some were shot with tranquilizer darts but swam away and drowned. Other animals became entangled in nets and were seriously wounded. The orcas that survived arduous journeys to marine parks often died or had to be put to sleep because few people knew how to care for them properly under artificial conditions. In fact, before 1970 more than 50 percent of all captive orcas died within two years of their capture. Of the other half, some managed to live for ten years and several survived for twenty years.

Capturing other cetaceans

While killer whales remain some of the most popular attractions at marine parks, smaller cetaceans such as bottlenose dolphins are also displayed. And unlike killer whales, these dolphins are relatively simpler to capture and transport, as Jerye Mooney explains in *Captive Cetaceans: A Handbook for Campaigners:*

> Resident Atlantic bottlenose dolphins have been captured with relative ease in the shallow waters of Florida and the Gulf of Mexico. Methods of capture in shallow waters utilise two high-speed boats—one for encircling the animals with a seine net, and another for transport equipment. A spotter plane is occasionally used to locate the animals. Once the "set" is complete, a smaller net is positioned inside the circle, further restricting animal movement, and drawn within 33 to 39 feet . . . in diameter. As the net closes, dolphins usually begin to strike the net, increasing the likelihood of entanglement and drowning. Entangled animals are recovered first, pulled aboard, measured, [their sex is determined], and [they are] physically examined. . . . [The] animals are selected according to needs; larger animals for breeding purposes, younger animals of three to five years of age, for training. . . . The number of animals accidentally killed

during capture operations remains unknown; reporting requirements [to the National Marine Fisheries Service] based on the
"honour system" remain questionable.[32]

Other species of dolphins are captured with more violent methods. The Pacific white-sided dolphin weighs
about three hundred pounds and is known as a "bow-rider"
because it likes to swim in the wake created by a speedboat. To capture white-sided dolphins, a hunter stands on a
platform that extends from his boat over the ocean. As the
boat speeds along next to a dolphin, the hunter places a
hoop net in front of the animal as it jumps out of the water
to catch a breath. When the dolphin is caught, the net
breaks and tangles around the animal. The entire apparatus
is attached to a rope that allows it to be pulled close to the
boat and raised on deck in a sling.

At one thousand to three thousand pounds, beluga whales
are about one-quarter the size of orcas. Their bizarre method
of capture is described by Mooney:

> Since 1967, beluga whales have been captured exclusively by
> the firm Nanuk Enterprises of Hudson Bay, using a unique
> and questionable capture method. Participants in the round-
> up have been called "cold water cowboys" for chasing belu-
> gas into shallow waters with speedboats, roping them, and
> literally jumping upon their backs to wrestle them into sub-
> mission rodeo-style.[33]

After the animals are harassed in this manner, they tire and
submit to being loaded on slings and hauled into boats.

Life in a tank

Researchers believe that capturing a dolphin or killer
whale in the open sea and putting it in a relatively small
tank is quite traumatic for the animal. As Canadian biolo-
gist Ian MacAskie says: "There'd be quite an outcry if a
dog were kept in a cage of the same relative size."[34]

The quality of care for the animals varies depending on
the facility. The most humane marine parks keep their animals in family groups contained by large netted enclosures
directly in the sea. As *Whales, Dolphins, and Porpoises*
states:

Filled naturally with seawater, and flushed with every new tide, these are often several acres in size and are deep enough for a reasonable amount of diving and swimming. The animals are fed a varied selection of fish, as well as vitamin and mineral supplements, and have regular checkups by experienced vets.[35]

Beluga whales are shown performing for tourists. Unfortunately, the methods used to capture belugas are often cruel and harmful to the animals.

These dolphin-friendly oceanariums stand in contrast to facilities that keep their cetaceans in bare, indoor, concrete tanks filled with dirty water. These animals cannot follow their natural instincts to hunt, dive, or use their echolocation.

Although humans can never know the exact feelings of the captive dolphins, the animals indicate stress through

Cetaceans in Captivity

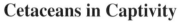

The OrcaInfo website (http://members.aol.com/OrcaInfo/page9.htm) lists some injuries to small whales and dolphins as a result of the animals' captivity in marine parks and oceanariums:

Marineland, Canada (1967): Less than a month after arriving at Marineland Canada from California, a pilot whale known as "Baby Jane" was described as having suicidal tendencies. She charged head-on into metal holding bars while being prepared for a medical examination. The whale reportedly had "smashed into the wall of the tank with blood gushing from a gash in her head, withered wildly about and almost threw her massive body out of the water."

Miami Seaquarium, Florida (1970s): Orca "Hugo" broke observation window, causing significant water loss and slicing off the end of his nose. . . .

Sea Life Park, Hawaii (1977): "Auwaha," a *Stenella* dolphin, was found the morning of April 2, 1977 out of the tank in the direct sun. Necropsy report concluded accidental death caused by traumatic injury and heat exhaustion. . . .

Marineland of the Pacific, California (1985): "Corky" broke observation window resulting in the loss of more than one-third water volume in tank. . . .

Gulfarium, Florida (1985): June 4 - "Sampson," an Atlantic bottlenose dolphin, died from "shock during treatment" six weeks after breaking an observation window and being sucked out over the broken glass, sustaining severe lacerations of the abdominal wall.

Dolphin Research Center, Florida (1987): After an attack by a larger male dolphin, the five-month-old bottlenose dolphin "Halley" was swimming erratically, bumping into objects and walls. Found dead three days after the attack, the necropsy report revealed severe trauma to both eyes, approximately 300 14 to 20 cm lacerations/punctures over the entire body, severe contusions and internal bleeding. The aggressive animal broke through several fence barriers to enter Halley's pool.

their behavior. They circle endlessly as if searching for a means of escape. They stop "talking" and may aggressively attack their trainers or each other. Some injure themselves by banging into the tank walls, and there are even reports of animals committing suicide in this manner. In *Marine Mammals and Man*, Forrest G. Wood writes about the behavior of a Dall's porpoise at a marine research center:

> When released in our 50 foot tank the porpoise swam directly into the wall. . . . [A]fter about half an hour of this kind of behavior it was caught and put in a harness to which a leash was attached. An attendant could then usually deflect the porpoise before it struck the side of the tank. Finally, the leash was attached to a makeshift [cord] fastened to the midpoint of a rope stretched tautly across the tank. The porpoise could then swim in circles without running into the wall and without becoming entangled. The animal had already injured itself, however, and died sometime in the early morning hours. [Our] veterinarian conducted a postmortem examination and concluded the death was due to trauma and hemorrhaging caused by the beating the porpoise sustained as it tried to swim through the wall and floor of the tank.[36]

Performing tricks

Dolphins that manage to survive at marine parks are often trained to perform a wide variety of tricks. People who train dolphins to execute such feats generally believe that these public displays not only mentally stimulate the animals but keep them physically fit. Those who oppose such exhibitions argue that the animals are forced to act in an unnatural manner. *Whales, Dolphins, and Porpoises* states:

> Animal welfare groups argue that [dolphin shows] do little more than perpetuate the manipulative attitude we have towards nature. Without a doubt, some shows can be very demeaning—with trainers riding around on the animals' backs, for example—and onlookers inevitably leave with the wrong impression of cetacean behavior in the wild and their "natural" relationship with humans.[37]

Those who produce such shows sometimes provide educational commentary that explains the biology and habitat of the dolphins. Other facilities, however, provide little educational information or imply that the animals are happy to live in captivity and would perform such tricks in a natural environment.

There are no easy answers to the question of keeping dolphins in captivity. While individual animals may suffer, conscientious marine parks such as Sea World provide a percentage of their profits for cetacean research and conservation. These facilities also allow tens of millions of people to observe these magnificent creatures firsthand. Without oceanariums and aquariums many of these people would never be able to observe dolphins at all.

Military use of dolphins

Many dolphins taken into captivity are sold to marine parks. A large number of these animals, however, have been sold to the U.S. Navy since the 1960s for top secret dolphin research. Dolphins have been trained to search out underwater mines, put tracking devices on hostile ships, and deliver bombs to enemy submarines. Animals equipped with underwater video cameras have been trained to guard military installations. And there are rumors that dolphins have even been trained to kill enemy divers.

The United States is not the only country that has enlisted dolphins in the national defense. Such practices have also taken place in the Soviet Union and other countries with records of hostility toward the United States. Although information about the U.S. military dolphin programs was classified for reasons of national security, after the collapse of the Soviet Union some of the facts came to light.

Between 1960 and 2000 the U.S. Navy worked with nearly four hundred dolphins and about a dozen beluga whales. In the early 1960s, the hydrodynamic qualities of dolphin bodies were studied in order to design faster torpedoes. The animals were also studied to help the navy overcome physical obstacles to deep-sea diving.

By the 1980s dolphins were used for two basic missions known as "search and recovery" and "swimmer diversion." Search-and-recovery missions are carried out by camera-equipped dolphins that are trained to retrieve fired test weapons or locate lost munitions underwater.

Procaptivity Views

While a large percentage of marine researchers and biologists oppose oceanariums, polls have shown that a majority of Americans feel that zoos and aquariums are essential to education and provide some of the only opportunities for people to see wild animals. In an interview with the TV show *Frontline* (available at www.pbs.org/wgbh/pages/frontline/shows/whales/debate/procap.html), Jim McBain, director of veterinary medicine at Sea World, describes why he approves of keeping cetaceans in captivity:

> I think that as our population becomes more and more crowded, more people are urbanized . . . there's less natural contact with animals living in the wild. I don't think that it's rational for us to assume that people are going to be able to get experiences with wild animals by all going into the wild, there's too many of us, we'll destroy what little habitat is left by trying to do that.

> I actually calculated once how many boat trips it would take to take all the Sea World guests that come to Sea World each year out to see killer whales [in the wild], and it was over two thousand boat trips a day. . . . Well, that would be ludicrous. So I think the mandate for the future, if [we] want a public that's knowledgeable about wild animals and has some sensitivity about them, if we want our children to have a chance to see many of these animals, it's gonna have to be in places like Sea World and the rest of the zoos in the world. These are gonna be the places where people are gonna be able to get in touch with nature without destroying habitat.

Many believe that aquariums are beneficial because for many people, they provide the only opportunity to see marine wildlife.

Swimmer-diversion missions use dolphins that are placed in cages in water surrounding military bases. When a dolphin sees a swimmer enter the area, it presses a button in the cage to alert a shore base that sends out boats and divers. The cages are opened by remote control from the base, and the dolphins approach the diver. Meanwhile, positioning devices attached to the dolphins' backs broadcast the animals' exact location. When naval divers arrive they rendezvous with the dolphins, who tow them to the location of the enemy diver. Dolphins can also be equipped with guns or other devices to kill the enemy.

Since dolphins could also be used by enemies of the United States, naval programs were developed to neutralize these possible threats. One lieutenant commander for the Naval Reserve outlined this strategy:

Since the 1960s, the U.S. Navy has used specially trained dolphins to carry out a variety of missions.

In a hostile confrontation, both sides will have to consider dolphins as potential enemy . . . weapons. In some situations, there may be no choice except to destroy dolphins or any marine mammal presenting a similar threat. Such a precedent could result in unpredictable intrusions into the ocean environment. For example, it may be a sound tactical decision to protect shipping in a harbor by poisoning the surrounding waters to remove the threat of dolphin attacks which would, coincidentally, remove a sizable portion of the area's ecology.[38]

While animal rights activists question the morality of such missions, researchers have reported over the years that dolphins have often been mistreated or physically abused for failing to perform their duties. In 1989 fifteen animal rights organizations took the U.S. Navy to court to stop it from using dolphins at a nuclear submarine base in Washington state. The lawsuit claimed that using trained dolphins as killers was life-threatening to the animals and so violated federal statutes. They also claimed that the navy's collection practices were depleting dolphin populations in specific regions. In addition, many of the animals were becoming sick or dying in captivity. The lawsuit was eventually thrown out of court, however, because the military claimed their program was exempt from environmental laws for reasons of national security.

Although the Cold War between the United States and the Soviet Union ended in 1990, military research with dolphins continues. The extent and the scope of the programs remain classified information.

Capturing continues

Although the military is exempt from such rules, the United States began restricting killer whale collection for oceanariums in 1972 with the passage of the Marine Mammal Protection Act. Canada soon enacted similar laws to protect orcas, and around this time researchers proved that the collectors had indeed been endangering entire pods of killer whales in the Pacific Northwest.

Under the new regulations, collectors had to file for special permits and follow strict rules. Humane collection methods were detailed and the numbers of animals allowed to be taken were limited. These new rules, however, simply caused collectors to move out of North American waters. By 1980 a healthy young orca could bring a price of three hundred thousand dollars to fishermen in Iceland and Japan.

In the 1990s, the controversy surrounding wild orca capture had grown to the point that many marine parks discontinued the practice. By this time, the largest oceanariums had successful programs to breed killer whales in captivity.

The growing commercial demand for killer whales, however, continued to fuel controversy. In 1997, ten orcas were trapped by Japanese fishermen near Taiji. In spite of protests from international environmental groups, several of the animals were sold for nearly half a million dollars each to a new Japanese marine park.

Marine parks are not the most serious threat that orcas face. The growing awareness of the stress placed on the animals, however, has caused a vocal minority to demand that all orcas in captivity be given their freedom. With tens of millions of people flocking to the marine parks and hundreds of millions of dollars in profits to be made, there is little doubt that the controversy will continue.

5

Saving the Dolphins

DOLPHINS FACE SERIOUS threats around the globe from fishing nets, pollution, habitat destruction, and other problems. While many species are endangered by these problems, dolphins are fortunate because they engender love and respect, which makes people more willing to save them.

Even as far back as the 1960s, when today's widespread environmental movement was in its infancy, people realized that something had to be done to save these graceful marine mammals. Since that time national governments and international environmental organizations have passed laws, placed observers on fishing boats, and organized embargoes and protests to protect cetaceans in almost every region of the globe.

Purse seine protection

The first movement to save dolphins and porpoises began in 1969 when William Perrin, a young scientist working for the U.S. National Marine Fisheries Service, rode along with a tuna fleet that was catching yellowfin with purse-seine nets in the Eastern Tropical Pacific (ETP). Perrin observed thousands of dolphins being killed and through further research determined that up to 250,000 were killed annually in this one region alone.

Perrin published his findings in a widely distributed report that quickly generated public outrage in the United States. As a result of intense lobbying by environmental groups, Congress passed the U.S. Marine Mammal Protection Act (MMPA) of

1972, landmark legislation that restricted killing, capturing, or harassing dolphins and porpoises.

The MMPA set quotas that progressively reduced the number of dolphins allowed to be killed each year in fishing nets. In 1976, for instance, 78,000 dolphins were allowed to be taken by the tuna fisheries. By 1981 the number was reduced to 20,500.

The law, however, was difficult to enforce. At the time the bill was written, 90 percent of the entire ETP fishing fleet was owned by companies based in the United States. When the bill was enacted, about three-quarters of the vessels had reregistered under flags of foreign nations that had

Dolphins engender widespread love and respect, inspiring people to save them.

no such restrictions in place. Since that time, a majority of boats in the ETP tuna fleet, whether or not they are owned by American companies, have been registered to Mexico, Venezuela, Ecuador, Panama, Korea, and other countries.

Although the MMPA is not enforced by these nations, environmental groups managed to persuade some fleets to use a process known as "backdown," in which edges of purse-seine nets are pushed down to allow dolphins to escape.

"Dolphin-safe" tuna

Even with backdown procedures in place, about 130,000 dolphins died in the ETP in 1986. In 1990, pressure by environmental groups forced Congress to enact the Dolphin Protection Consumer Information Act (DPCIA). This law asked tuna canners to voluntarily stop buying yellowfin caught with purse-seine nets.

Responding to the law and widespread public pressure, the three largest U.S. tuna processors announced that they would only buy "dolphin-safe" tuna and that they would label their product with a special logo. Consumer response was so positive that smaller canners switched to dolphin-safe tuna to increase sales.

In 1991 Congress augmented the DPCIA, doing away with the voluntary measures and making it illegal for any U.S. citizen to encircle dolphins or sell tuna that was not dolphin safe.

This new legislation, however, conflicted with U.S. trade policy that was supposed to allow unrestricted imports from countries such as Mexico where purse-seine nets were still in use. While diplomats fielded formal protests from these countries, many fisheries switched from yellowfin to smaller tuna species in order to avoid the controversy. The drift-net methods used to catch the smaller tuna, however, were deadly to endangered sea turtles, birds, and sharks, along with other species that swam with the smaller fish.

In reaction to that problem, Congress passed the International Dolphin Conservation Program Act (IDCPA) that allowed fishermen to use purse seines once again but to use

Pinging Away Porpoises

Most people who make their living from the sea do not want to kill dolphins and porpoises along with their bycatch. According to a January 6, 1999, article by Marla Cone in the *Los Angeles Times*, one inventive fisherman devised a way to save cetaceans across the globe:

> Erik Anderson, who has fished New England's waters for 30 years, would haul up his gill net and occasionally discover a harbor porpoise, entangled and dying, trapped in the mesh along with his harvest of cod and flounder. . . .

> Up to 2,000 of the animals were drowning in gill nets in the Gulf of Maine each year—enough to eventually wipe out the species. And if nothing was done soon to stop it, the already struggling fishery would be shut down by federal authorities. . . .

> Following a hunch about acoustics from a Canadian whale behaviorist a few years ago, Anderson and some of his colleagues started experimenting with their nets.

> At Radio Shack, they purchased a batch of the devices that sound a beep on school buses when they back up. They tied the bulky boxes onto their gill nets, and set them into the Gulf of Maine. . . . [Amazingly], porpoises heard the low-frequency alarms and avoided swimming into the nets.

> Now, word is spreading around the globe, fisherman to fisherman. Ping, ping, ping can be heard in ocean waters from South Africa to the Irish Sea.

> Called "pingers," net alarms are considered so successful in protecting marine mammals that a federal order recently mandated them on drift nets off California and Oregon and sink nets in New England.

> Deaths of whales and dolphins have dropped by two-thirds on the West Coast—with 90 common dolphins dying in 1997, compared with a past average of 271 annually. . . . On the East Coast, porpoise deaths in the Gulf of Maine have declined by more than 90%.

intensified backdown methods. Although some environmentalists worry about the psychological harm suffered by animals caught and then released, researchers report that trapped dolphins have learned to wait patiently for their captors to free them. By 1998, countries such as Mexico, hoping to improve their international standing, began the widespread use of backdown methods. In that year a record low of 2,700 dolphins were killed in the ETP.

Meanwhile the search continues for new yellowfin fishing methods that are completely dolphin safe. As *The Greenpeace Book of Dolphins* states: "It is now known, for example, that tuna will congregate under virtually any floating object. Fish Aggregating Devices (FADs), rafts beneath which fish gather, are already being used on a trial basis in some parts of the world."[39] Research continues and activists hope to lower the numbers of dolphins killed by tuna fishermen to near zero.

Stopping drift nets

While purse-seine nets can be restricted or used in a manner that harms fewer dolphins, drift nets act as aquatic vacuum cleaners, sucking up every living creature in their path, 25 percent of which is unwanted bycatch. Dolphins continue to face serious threats from the hundreds of thousands of miles of these nets floating around in the world's oceans. And the destruction caused by drift nets has been obvious to researchers and environmentalists since the nets first came into use in the early 1980s.

It was not until June 11, 1989, however, that the first regulations against drift nets were put into place. At that time, the South Pacific Forum, made up of countries such as Australia, New Zealand, Fiji, Samoa, Tahiti, and other island nations in the region, enacted a strict ban against the use of drift nets in their waters. By issuing a document known as the Tarawa Declaration, the forum called on Japan and Taiwan to ban the use of these nets.

Following the example of the South Pacific Forum, the United Nations General Assembly passed a resolution in December 1989 calling for the phaseout of drift nets. In

Pictured are tuna captured in a purse-seine net. It is possible for purse seines to be restricted or used in a manner that harms fewer dolphins.

1992 the UN declared a moratorium on all drift netting in the high seas. That same year France, Germany, Italy, the Netherlands, and other countries of the European Union (EU) moved to limit drift-net length in the Mediterranean Sea to about 1.5 miles each. These regulations were poorly enforced, however, and in 1998 at least six hundred Italian fishing boats were found to be using drift nets up to 12 miles in length.

In a case of environmental groups forcing governments to take action, Greenpeace International sent observers out to document evidence that drift-net regulations were being ignored. After dodging bullets and knives from angry Italian fishermen, observers managed to gather photographic and physical evidence including several drift nets that were taken from an Italian boat that reached 162 miles in length.

 ## The Tarawa Declaration

On June 11,1989, the South Pacific Forum issued the Tarawa Declaration to ban Taiwan and Japan from using drift-net fishing in the region. The official declaration was posted on the University of the South Pacific School of Law website (www.vanuatu.usp.ac.fj):

TARAWA DECLARATION

Recognizing the crucial dependence of the Pacific Island peoples on marine resources,

Profoundly concerned at the damage now being done by [oceanic] drift-net fishing to the economy and environment of the South Pacific region,

Convinced that this indiscriminate, irresponsible and destructive fishing technique threatens the survival of the albacore tuna resource, and so the economic well-being of Forum Island Countries,

Deeply regretting that Japan and Taiwan have failed to respond to the concerns of regional countries about this most serious issue,

Noting that it is in the mutual interest of the major fishing nations active in the region, and the Forum, to conserve fisheries stocks,

Noting also that all countries inside and outside the region are affected by the mismanagement of the resources of the world's oceans, by the environmental dangers of drift-net fishing and by the threat to safe navigation. . . .

Recognizing that the use of drift nets as presently employed in the Southern Pacific Albacore Tuna Fishery is not consistent with international legal requirements in relation to rights and obligations of high seas fisheries conservation and management and environmental principles,

Resolves, for the sake of this and succeeding generations of Pacific peoples, to seek the establishment of a régime for the management of albacore tuna in the South Pacific that would ban drift-net fishing from the region; such a ban might then be a first step to a comprehensive ban on such fishing. . . .

Calls upon Japan and Taiwan to follow this example, and abandon immediately their damaging drift-net operations.

The protesters took their findings to an EU Council meeting of fisheries ministers in Luxembourg and successfully lobbied the regulators to ban drift nets completely. In addition, tens of millions of dollars were put into a fund to compensate fishermen for switching to more environmentally friendly fishing methods.

Still, in spite of bans by the EU and the UN, drift-net fishing continues. Russia remains one of the few countries in the world that still permits large-scale drift-net fishing in its national waters. In June 2000 Greenpeace observers found abandoned "ghost" drift nets in Russian waters in which five endangered Dall's porpoises were drowned along with sharks, seabirds, and other threatened marine life. These nets were suspected to have come from fee-paying Japanese drift netters that Russia allows to fish its waters.

Saving the Yangtze River dolphin

Groups that have taken action to limit purse-seine and drift-net fishing have saved countless dolphins and porpoises. And while regulating fishing boats is still a difficult task, efforts have been generally successful. Those who want to save river dolphins, however, face a much bigger challenge because these animals live in extremely polluted waters and highly populated areas.

The tragic fate of river dolphins prompted researchers and environmentalists to hold a meeting in China in 1986 to search for new ways to save the animals. Several methods were discussed, including habitat conservation and better river management.

After the meeting China granted the Yangtze River dolphin, or baiji, official status as Protected Animal of the First Order, placing it in the same category as the endangered giant panda. Using newspapers, magazines, movies, and even a baiji postage stamp, the government embarked on a widespread campaign to educate the local population about the threats to the river dolphins. To coordinate the efforts, an organization called the Baiji Conservation Associations formed clubs at various points along the Yangtze. The associations' volunteer members educate fishermen

and others who work on the river about the plight of the river dolphin.

This campaign was given a further boost when the association convinced a local brewery to put the baiji on its label so people would be interested in finding out more about the animal. Other companies joined in the campaign, and the Yangtze region now has products such as shoes, fertilizer, computerized weighing scales, and even toilet paper all containing the baiji advertising logo. As a result the baiji and its environmental problems have become familiar to millions in the region.

The Chinese government has also tried to save the dolphins by closing off a section of the Yangtze between two islets to form a seminatural reserve for the baiji. The reserve at Tongling contains a hospital for treating sick or hurt baiji and facilities for studying the animals while in captivity. Animals are kept there for a time and later released back into their natural environment. Unfortunately, fewer than 100

Although it was granted official status as Protected Animal of the First Order by the Chinese government, the Yangtze River dolphin is still threatened by pollution and fishermen's nets and hooks.

Yangtze River Dolphin Preserve

The Yangtze River dolphin, or baiji, is a beloved animal in China. Through a public education campaign, many are aware of its plight and hope to save it from extinction. The Yangtze is very polluted, however, and researchers are taking measures to save the baiji, as detailed in this December 5, 1997, *Los Angeles Times* article by Rone Tempest:

> Conditions in the Yangtze River are so inhospitable for the dolphin that biologists have given up trying to improve the river habitat to save the species. Instead, they have concentrated their efforts in a last-ditch effort to create a "semi-natural preserve" for the remaining dolphins in an oxbow [U-shaped bend] of the river at Shishou, about 150 miles upriver from Wuhan.
>
> The latest rescue plan is to net and capture the remaining dolphins and transport them to the Shishou oxbow. The biologists were hopeful in 1995 when they managed to capture a female dolphin and place her in the reserve. But the first effort ended in disaster less than a year later when the female died after becoming snagged in the net separating the reserve from the main river.
>
> Since then, the Chinese government's river-dolphin program has begun construction of a concrete-and-steel-mesh fence that poses less threat to the dolphins but still allows water and fish to enter.

baiji are left alive in the wild, and attempts to breed them in captivity have been disappointing.

Freeing Keiko

Most researchers believe that the Yangtze River dolphin may survive only if kept in captivity. In other countries, activists want to take dolphins that are already in captivity and release them into the wild. This movement was given widespread publicity in 1993 when the movie *Free Willy,* about an orca that escapes from a marine park, was released in theaters.

Free Willy starred a killer whale named Keiko who was born around 1978 in the North Atlantic near Iceland. When he was a calf barely two years old he was caught in a net by herring fishermen and eventually sold to a Canadian marine park. Put in a tank with six other orcas, Keiko was timid and difficult to train. In 1985 Keiko was sold to an amusement park in Mexico City where he was put in a small tank with bottlenose dolphins and sea lions and forced to perform five shows a day.

At the end of *Free Willy*, a toll-free number was displayed on the screen that filmgoers could call if they wanted to help free the movie's star. More than three hundred thousand people from all over the world called the number. Schoolchildren organized campaigns, and *Life* magazine ran a cover story to help "free Willy."

By the time the film was released Keiko's health was severely compromised by his captivity. His immune system was weak, leaving him open to many types of infectious diseases. He was also severely underweight and his muscles had atrophied from living in a small tank.

As calls poured in to free Keiko, the overwhelmed Mexico City amusement park began efforts to relocate their now-famous orca. As the search for a new home for Keiko began, Sea World donated several refrigerated coolers to lower the orca's tank temperature from its unhealthy eighty degrees Fahrenheit to a more comfortable mid-sixties.

Remarkable recovery

In 1995 the Free Willy Keiko Foundation was formed, and the nonprofit group raised enough money to move the ailing orca to a rehabilitation facility at the Oregon Coast Aquarium in Newport, Oregon.

Keiko was placed in a much larger tank that was filled with cold sea water. In his years of captivity Keiko had lost many of his natural abilities to survive in the open sea. His natural curiosity was blunted and he showed little interest in his new surroundings. Keiko was unable to dive for long periods at a time because he could only hold his breath for three minutes instead of the normal fifteen. And a viral infection had given him large, warty tissue masses around his flippers and tail flukes.

Keiko was put under the care of a veterinarian who practiced holistic, or natural, medicine that focused on improving the health of the animal's body, mind, and spirit. Keiko was nursed back to health with a program of cardiovascular workouts, a better diet, interaction with other members of his species, and mental stimulation to bring him out of his depression.

By 1996 Keiko had gained over one thousand pounds, lost most of his skin lesions, was able to hold his breath for thirteen minutes, and was mentally alert and playful. Keiko's amazing recovery startled nearly everyone who worked with him.

For the next two years Keiko was taught to catch fish. In September 1998, after having spent nineteen years of his life in captivity, the twenty-one-year-old orca was flown to Iceland and placed in a large pen built specially

After his amazing recovery, Keiko (pictured) was flown to a pen in Iceland in anticipation of his eventual release.

for him in the North Atlantic. Although he was not immediately released into the wild, his handlers continue to hope that he will ultimately be able to gain his freedom in the open sea.

While millions of dollars have been spent rehabilitating the famous killer whale, at least a dozen wild orcas continue to be taken into captivity every year. The publicity given to Keiko's plight, however, helped raise money and awareness for other threatened cetaceans.

Marine sanctuaries

Keiko's rehabilitation is taking place in a protected marine sanctuary where he is able to live in safety. While Keiko has his own private sanctuary, there are dozens of other such places across the globe where pods of dolphins thrive under government protection.

The United States is a leader in creating marine sanctuaries. In 1972, the same year that the Marine Mammal Protection Act was passed, Congress also passed the National Marine Protection, Research and Sanctuaries Act to establish protected areas in America's territorial waters.

The act was originally designed to prevent unregulated dumping in the oceans, but it also called on government agencies to manage marine sites based on ecological, recreational, historical, scenic, or educational value. Since that time thirteen marine sanctuaries have been created in America's coastal waters, including the Olympic coast in Washington State, Monterey Bay in California, and areas of the Florida Keys. All of these areas are within habitats for many species of dolphins and porpoises as well as other threatened marine life.

Following the lead of the United States, several other countries have authorized sanctuaries, some specifically designed to protect dolphins and porpoises. In 1992 the government of Brazil established a preserve on the southeastern coastal waters near Florianópolis to protect the threatened tucuxi dolphins that live only in that particular region.

In 1999 the governments of France, Italy, and Monaco announced that they would create an international marine sanctuary for whales and dolphins in the Mediterranean Sea. The protected region is in the waters that lie along the Riviera and the coast of Italy. The area, known as the Sanctuary for the Protection of the Cetaceans, makes up 4 percent of the Mediterranean and was put aside after a ten-year campaign by the international environmental organization World Wide Fund for Nature.

There are at least eighteen cetacean species living in the western Mediterranean. Of the dolphins, several species, including the common, bottlenose, and Risso's dolphins, are permanent residents that live there all year. In the summer as many as fifty thousand striped dolphins and two thousand whales come into the area when there is an abundance of the tiny crustaceans that make up their diet.

In this officially designated sanctuary, laws prevent the harassment of marine mammals by tourist boats. They also ban drift-net fishing and speedboat competitions, and expand efforts to control pollution.

Individuals working for dolphins

Officially sanctioned marine preserves have allowed the growth of dolphin research centers near such areas. These facilities, in turn, have attracted thousands of tourists who gladly pay to ride along on dolphin- and whale-watching expeditions to observe the animals in their natural environment. Some of these profitable cruises are even run by former fishermen who were forced to quit fishing because of gill-net bans or declining fish populations.

The book *Whales, Dolphins, and Porpoises* explains how such concessions help cetaceans:

> Responsible whale watching provides opportunities for photography, study and enjoyment of a wide range of cetaceans. The growing popularity of whale watching—from the shore, from small boats or from organized commercial trips—has encouraged some countries to introduce guidelines that seek to protect the whales from intrusion, harassment and exploitation. Quietly observing the natural behavior of cetaceans without disturbing their activities is surely of greater value than watching them perform tricks in a theme park.[40]

Saving White Dolphins

The white dolphins that live in the busy and polluted waters near Hong Kong are facing extinction. This May 15, 2000, article by Andrea Pawlyna on the Environmental News Network (ENN) website (www.enn.com) explains what is being done to save them:

Threatened by pollution, shipping traffic and overfishing, only 80 to 140 dolphins remain in Hong Kong's waters.

Last month, the government's Department of Agriculture, Fisheries and Conservation began "planting" artificial reefs in the hope that they will eventually attract enough fish to satisfy the dolphins' diet.

Twenty-four aging river barges, 42 container units and thousands of hollow concrete blocks are being sunk in Sha Chau and Lung Kwu Chau Marine Park at a cost of . . . $650,000. Artificial reefs attract colonies of marine organisms, which in turn provide a source of food for fish.

"Dolphins frequent that area and we expect them to use the site a lot more now that the artificial reefs have been put down," said Keith Wilson, senior fisheries officer for the department.

Artificial reefs are not new, but this is believed to be the first time they have been deployed for the benefit of dolphins. . . .

Admired for its features, the Hong Kong white dolphin faces extinction because of pollution.

Hong Kong's dolphins belong to the Indo-Pacific humpbacked species, which is widely distributed from South Africa to Australia to the Chinese coast of the Yangtze River. But what has made these particular dolphins, as well as populations in the South China Sea and Southeast Asia, such a favorite of admirers is their coloring.

Born nearly black, the dolphins gradually become white or pink as they reach adulthood. Their striking pink body color appears almost rouge-like against the dark blue water as they leap and frolic in group formation.

While such expeditions are beneficial to tourists, some individuals have taken a more hands-on approach to helping dolphins and porpoises by saving animals that have accidentally washed ashore. In Brigantine, New Jersey, for example, the Marine Mammal Stranding Center—a private, nonprofit group—has helped hundreds of stranded dolphins and whales return to the sea. Sick or wounded animals are brought to the center for rehabilitation and eventual release. Such treatment can take several months and cost thousands of dollars per animal, and the center relies on donations to perform this expensive task. Since the group was founded in 1978 it has rescued an ever-increasing number of creatures, helping with 19 strandings its first year and more than 165 in 1999.

Those who volunteer for this group must live within fifteen minutes of the New Jersey shore and must attend workshops and training sessions given by the center. Similar organizations operate in Virginia and elsewhere.

Other efforts to help stranded dolphins are more spontaneous. In January 2000, about fifty bottlenose dolphins mysteriously stranded themselves in shallow waters off of Long Key, Florida. Local residents entered the rocky shallows where the dolphins were becoming scratched and scarred on the jagged sea floor. Forming a human chain more than a quarter-mile long, divers and snorkelers helped push about twenty of the stranded dolphins back out to sea.

Small efforts for big results

Not everyone can rescue stranded dolphins or take expensive whale-watching trips. Tens of thousands of people, however, have contributed to environmental organizations such as Greenpeace, the American Cetacean Society, the Whale and Dolphin Conservation Society, and others. Contributions average about twenty dollars, but every little bit helps in the fight to preserve dolphins and porpoises. These groups use their money to help enact environmental legislation, educate the public, and employ observers to keep a watchful eye over the practices of fishing fleets.

Most conservation groups are funded from private and corporate donations. The state of Florida, however, has come up with innovative ways to fund dolphin and porpoise protection. In 1999 the Florida Department of Motor Vehicles began selling Protect Wild Dolphins license plates for cars. For a twenty-dollar annual fee motorists can get a beautiful license plate featuring a jumping dolphin silhouetted by the rising sun. The money from the plates funds dolphin research and education programs that focus on the preservation of wild dolphins. The program is administered by the Harbor Branch Oceanographic Institution, whose president, Rick Herman, said:

> It is immensely fitting that Florida . . . [which relies on the tourist business has] designated the Protect Wild Dolphins license plate to fund the protection and well-being of this most exquisite, friendly and intelligent animal. The future of wild dolphins—currently on the federal protected species list—is now significantly brighter.[41]

Florida's Protect Wild Dolphins license plate program is just one of many campaigns designed to ensure the survival of dolphins and porpoises.

Programs such as the dolphin license plates in Florida are just one piece of a complicated puzzle researchers, marine biologists, environmentalists, and average people are putting together to protect and save dolphins and porpoises. Few people care to imagine a world where there is no place for playful dolphins to frolic, unharmed, in the sea. But as the world becomes more populated, and human needs affect even the most remote regions of the world's oceans, many measures need to be taken to save marine mammals. If each individual added one small piece, however, then the planet Earth would always include the seventy-nine species of dolphins and porpoises that have been here for millions of years.

Notes

Introduction

1. Quoted in "Earth Almanac," *National Geographic*, May 1991, p. 142.
2. Kenneth S. Norris, "Dolphins in Crisis," *National Geographic*, September 1992, p. 13.

Chapter 1: Rulers of the Sea

3. Jean-Pierre Sylvestre, *Dolphins and Porpoises*. New York: Sterling Publishing, 1993, p. 11.
4. Ben Wilson, *Dolphins of the World*. Stillwater, MN: Voyageur Press, 1998, p. 17.
5. Wilson, *Dolphins of the World*, p. 18.
6. Jacques-Yves Cousteau and Philippe Diolé, *Dolphins*. New York: Arrowood Press, 1987, pp. 172–73.
7. Wilson, *Dolphins of the World*, pp. 25–26.
8. Norris, "Dolphins in Crisis," p. 11.
9. Wilson, *Dolphins of the World*, p. 29.
10. Cousteau and Diolé, *Dolphins*, pp. 175–76.
11. John May, ed., *The Greenpeace Book of Dolphins*. New York: Sterling Publishing, 1990, p. 26.
12. May, *The Greenpeace Book of Dolphins*, p. 28.

Chapter 2: Threats from Fishing and Hunting

13. May, *The Greenpeace Book of Dolphins*, p. 96.
14. Norris, "Dolphins in Crisis," p. 18.
15. "Indiscriminate Slaughter at Sea," National Audubon Society, www.audubon.org/campaign/lo/ow/iss.html.
16. "Indiscriminate Slaughter at Sea."
17. Peter G. H. Evans, *The Natural History of Whales and Dolphins*. New York: Facts On File, 1987, p. 256.
18. Norris, "Dolphins in Crisis," p. 8.
19. Norris, "Dolphins in Crisis," p. 8.

20. Hardy Jones, "The Futo Dolphin Massacre," www.dolphin link.com/alert/futomas.html, October 2000.

21. May, *The Greenpeace Book of Dolphins*, p. 91.

Chapter 3: Pollution and Habitat Destruction

22. May, *The Greenpeace Book of Dolphins*, p. 109.

23. Quoted in Norris, "Dolphins in Crisis," p. 20.

24. Nadeem Iqbal, "Pakistan's Pollution Levels Making Indus Dolphin Infertile," www.woza.co.za/eco/news/sep00/dolphin 13.htm, September 2000.

25. May, *The Greenpeace Book of Dolphins*, p. 111.

26. Norris, "Dolphins in Crisis," p. 18.

27. Quoted in May, *The Greenpeace Book of Dolphins*, p. 119.

28. May, *The Greenpeace Book of Dolphins*, p. 119.

Chapter 4: Dolphins and Porpoises in Captivity

29. Quoted in "Quotes," http://members.aol.com/Orca Info/page9.htm, 1999.

30. Quoted in Jerye Mooney, *Captive Cetaceans: A Handbook for Campaigners*. Bath, England: Whale and Dolphin Conservation Society, 1998, p. 11.

31. May, *The Greenpeace Book of Dolphins*, p. 134.

32. Mooney, *Captive Cetaceans*, p. 10.

33. Mooney, *Captive Cetaceans*, p. 10.

34. Quoted in "Quotes," http://members.aol.com/Orca Info/page9.htm, 1999.

35. Mark Carwardine, ed., *Whales, Dolphins, and Porpoises*. New York: Checkmark Books, 1999, p. 198.

36. Forrest G. Wood, *Marine Mammals and Man*. Washington, DC: B. Luce, 1973, pp. 41–42.

37. Carwardine, *Whales, Dolphins, and Porpoises*, p. 199.

38. Quoted in May, *The Greenpeace Book of Dolphins*, p. 129.

Chapter 5: Saving the Dolphins

39. May, *The Greenpeace Book of Dolphins*, p. 99.

40. Carwardine, *Whales, Dolphins, and Porpoises*, p. 203.

41. Quoted in Environmental News Network, "Dolphin License Plates on Sale in Florida," www.enn.com/enn-news-archive/1999/04/041999/dolphin_2719.asp, April 19, 1999.

Organizations
to Contact

American Cetacean Society
PO Box 1391
San Pedro, CA 90733
(310) 548-6279 or (310) 548-6279
e-mail: acs@pobox.com
website: www.acsonline.org/

The American Cetacean Society works to protect whales, dolphins, porpoises, and their habitats through education, conservation, and research.

American Oceans Campaign
725 Arizona Ave., Suite 102
Santa Monica, CA 90401
(310) 576-6162
e-mail: allianceam@aol.com
website: www.allianceforamerica.org/Oldweb/0199002.htm

Founded by actor Ted Danson, American Oceans Campaign's mission is to protect and preserve the vitality of coastal waters, estuaries, bays, wetlands, and deep oceans.

Center for Marine Conservation
Warner Chabot
580 Market St., Suite 550
San Francisco, CA 94104
(415) 391-6204
e-mail: cmc@dccmc.org
website: www.cmc-ocean.org/

The Center for Marine Conservation is committed to conserving the abundance and diversity of the world's marine life and protecting the health of the oceans and seas.

Cousteau Society
870 Greenbriar Cir., Suite 492
Chesapeake, VA 23320
(800) 441-4395
e-mail: cousteau@cousteausociety.org
website: www.cousteau.org/

Founded by the late ocean explorer Jacques-Yves Cousteau, the organization provides information and insight on environmental issues concerning the world's oceans.

Earth Island Institute, Inc.
300 Broadway, Suite 28
San Francisco, CA 94133
(415) 788-3666
e-mail: earthisland@earthisland.org
website: www.earthisland.org/home_body.cfm

This organization develops and supports projects that counteract threats to the biological and cultural diversity that sustain the environment. Through education and activism, these projects promote the conservation, preservation, and restoration of the earth.

Greenpeace
568 Howard St., 3rd Floor
San Francisco, CA 94105
(800) 326-0959 or (415) 512-9025
e-mail: supporter.services@ams.greenpeace.org
website: www.greenpeace.org

Greenpeace draws attention to abuses of the environment through their presence at the scene, whatever the risk.

Natural Resources Defense Council
40 W. 20th St.
New York, NY 10011
(212) 727-2700
e-mail: nrdcinfo@nrdc.org
website: www.nrdc.org/default.asp

The Natural Resources Defense Council uses law, science, and the support of more than four hundred thousand members nationwide to protect the planet's wildlife and wild places and to ensure a safe and healthy environment for all living things.

Ocean Futures

Ocean Futures Society
325 Chapala St.
Santa Barbara, CA 93101
(805) 899-8899
website: www.oceanfutures.org/

Ocean Futures is run by Jean-Michel Cousteau to provide the global community with a forum for exploring issues affecting the ocean, its inhabitants, and its habitats.

Whale and Dolphin Conservation Society

Alexander House,
James St. West,
Bath BA1 2BT
United Kingdom
e-mail: webmaster@wdcs.org
website: www.wdcs.org/dan/publishing.nsf/frontpagereadform

The Whale and Dolphin Conservation Society is dedicated to the conservation and welfare of all whales, dolphins, and porpoises.

Suggestions for Further Reading

Mark Carwardine, ed., *Whales, Dolphins, and Porpoises*. New York: Checkmark Books, 1999. A large, colorful book of cetacean biology and ecology with dozens of illustrations and incredible action photos.

Casey Horton, *Dolphins*. New York: Benchmark Books, 1996. Part of the *Endangered!* series, this young adult book explores species of dolphin that are severely threatened, including the killer whale, bottlenose dolphin, Chinese river dolphin, and others.

John May, ed., *The Greenpeace Book of Dolphins*. New York: Sterling Publishing, 1990. A book published by the Greenpeace environmental organization that explains the ecology of dolphins and lists threats to the animals in different environments around the globe.

Andrew Read, *Porpoises*. Stillwater, MN: Voyageur Press, 1999. A striking book that focuses on porpoise biology and ecology. Illustrated with many entertaining photographs.

Virginia Schomp, *The Bottlenose Dolphin*. New York: Dillon Press, 1994. Part of the Remarkable Animals series, this book is a detailed exploration of bottlenose dolphins and the threats they face in the wild.

Ben Wilson, *Dolphins of the World*. Stillwater, MN: Voyageur Press, 1998. An attractive, well-illustrated book that explores the beauty, biology, and mystery of dolphins.

Works Consulted

Books and Periodicals
Jacques-Yves Cousteau and Philippe Diolé, *Dolphins*. New York: Arrowood Press, 1987. Cousteau was the captain of the ocean research vessel *Calypso* and producer of dozens of award-winning films about the ocean and marine biology. This book on dolphins is based on years of firsthand research by one of the world's best-known explorers of the earth's undersea environment.

"Earth Almanac," *National Geographic*, May 1991. An article about a massive dolphin die-off caused by a virus in the Mediterranean.

Peter G. H. Evans, *The Natural History of Whales and Dolphins*. New York: Facts On File, 1987. A book that offers detailed analysis of physical characteristics, population numbers, and other natural history aspects of cetaceans.

John Lilly, *Man and Dolphin*. Garden City, NY: Doubleday, 1961. Dr. John Lilly is one of the world's foremost proponents of the controversial theory that dolphins are as smart as—or smarter than—humans. In this, his first book on the subject, Lilly details his experiments in communication with dolphins that later stimulated worldwide interest in the animals.

Kenneth S. Norris, *Dolphin Days*. New York: W. W. Norton, 1991. A book about spinner dolphins, their social interactions at sea, and their fate at the hands of humans. Written by a professor of natural history at the University of California, Santa Cruz, who has been studying dolphins and porpoises since 1950.

————, "Dolphins in Crisis," *National Geographic*, September 1992. An article about endangered dolphins in Japan, the United States, and elsewhere by a world-renowned cetacean expert.

Jean-Pierre Sylvestre, *Dolphins and Porpoises*. New York: Sterling Publishing, 1993. A field guide to dolphins and porpoises that includes common names, characteristics, population numbers, and field identification.

Jose Ma. Lorenzo Tan, *A Field Guide to Whales and Dolphins in the Philippines*. Makati City, Manila: Bookmark, 1995. A field guide with information about cetaceans in the Philippines along with important information dealing with the threats these animals are facing.

Forrest G. Wood, *Marine Mammals and Man*. Washington, DC: B. Luce, 1973. A book written by a researcher for the U.S. Navy concerning the use of porpoises and sea lions in various military experiments.

Internet Sources
Eugene H. Buck, "Dolphin Protection and Tuna Seining," Congressional Research Service Issue Brief Environment and Natural Resources Policy Division, www.cnie.org/nle/mar-14.html, August 29, 1997. A website with in-depth information regarding the history and details of laws covering purse-seine tuna fishing and the scope of the laws' influence on saving dolphins.

Marla Cone, "The 'Ping' Heard 'Round the World," *Los Angeles Times*, www.earth-in-balance.org/VOS/VOSS1.htm, January 6, 1999. An article about drift-net fishermen who attach loud pinging devices to their nets to repel dolphins and porpoises.

Environmental News Network, "Dolphin License Plates on Sale in Florida," www.enn.com/enn-news-archive/1999/04/041999/dolphin_2719.asp, April 19, 1999. An article on the

Environmental News Network (ENN) website explaining Florida's new dolphin license plate whose fee helps protect the animals in coastal waters. ENN is the largest and longest-running web portal that features environmental news.

Frontline Online, "A Whale of a Business," www.pbs.org/wgbh/pages/frontline/shows/whales/debate/procap.html, 1998. An interview with the vice president of zoological operations at Sea World in which the procaptivity views of those keeping cetaceans in oceanariums are discussed.

Nadeem Iqbal, "Pakistan's Pollution Levels Making Indus Dolphin Infertile," www.woza.co.za/eco/news/sep00/dolphin13.htm, September 2000. An article on the Eco website, based in South Africa, about the threats facing the susu in Pakistan.

Hardy Jones, "The Futo Dolphin Massacre," www.dolphinlink.com/alert/futomas.html, October 2000. This website associated with the Earth Island Institute Dolphin Link contains information about the capture and slaughter of dolphins in Futo Bay, Japan.

Jerye Mooney, *Captive Cetaceans: A Handbook for Campaigners*. Bath, England: Whale and Dolphin Conservation Society, www.wdcs.org/dan/publishing.nsf/(allweb)/7827FA2E2D3FF378802568F1002E340E, 1998. A "how-to" manual for those who wish to stop the capture and display of cetaceans at marine parks.

National Audubon Society, "Indiscriminate Slaughter at Sea," www.audubon.org/campaign/lo/ow/iss.html. A website that is part of the Audubon Society's Ocean Wildlife Campaign with numerous details about the hazards to wildlife from industrial fishing fleets.

National Marine Sanctuaries, www.sanctuaries.nos.noaa.gov/welcome.html, October 13, 2000. Information about the marine sanctuaries of the United States—how they were established, how they are managed, their scientific and educational programs, and the many exciting events that occur in them throughout the year.

National Resources Defense Council, "Navy Sonar System Threatens Marine Animals," www.nrdc.org/wildlife/marine/nlfa.asp, September 11, 2000. An article about the U.S. Navy's Low Frequency Active Sonar and its negative impact on whales and dolphins. Site includes an e-mail letter visitors can sign and send to the secretary of the navy to halt this project.

Andrea Pawlyna, "Artificial Reefs Will Benefit Hong Kong Dolphins," www.enn.com/enn-features-archive/2000/05/05152000/hkdolphin_11509.asp, May 15, 2000. An Environmental News Network article detailing steps being taken to save Hong Kong's threatened white dolphins.

"Quotes," http://members.aol.com/OrcaInfo/page9.htm, 1999. A page of quotes from "Orcas in Captivity," a website maintained by Jerye Mooney with many articles about the pain and trauma suffered by cetaceans in marine parks.

Rone Tempest, "Rare Yangtze River Dolphins Struggle for Survival," http://seattletimes.nwsource.com/extra/browse/html97/dolp_120597.html, *Los Angeles Times*, December 5, 1997. An article about the rare Yangtze River dolphins, the threats facing them, and the steps being taken to ensure their survival.

"Treaties and Conventions—Tarawa Declaration on Driftnet Fishing," www.vanuatu.usp.ac.fj/pactreaties/Treaties_etc/treaties_Tarawa_Declaration.html, February 13, 2000. A declaration that bans drift-net fishing in the South Pacific, posted on the University of the South Pacific School of Law website.

The Wild Dolphin Project, http://dolphin.wwwa.com/. Founded by Dr. Denise Herzing in 1985, the Wild Dolphin Project has been studying one group of Atlantic spotted dolphins in the Bahamas for more than fifteen years. While learning about dolphin behavior, communications, and interaction, the group has recorded ecological threats to the animals from fishing, pollution, and other sources.

Woods Hole Oceanographic Institution, www.whoi.edu/. According to its website, the Woods Hole Oceanographic Institution in Massachusetts is "the largest independent oceanographic institution in the world, and is a private, non-profit research facility dedicated to the study of marine science and to the education of marine scientists."

Index

algae, 55, 56–58
Amazon River, 48–50
Anderson, Erik, 78

babies, 20–22
backdown, 77
baiji, 48, 82–84
Baiji Conservation
  Associations, 82–83
beak, 10–11
behavior
  clicking, 16–20
  communication, 16–20
  diving, 15–16
  feeding, 14–15, 18
  fishing (hunting), 20, 25
  noise-making, 17–18, 24
  "running," 13–14
  sleeping, 23
  swimming, 11–12
belugas, 40, 63, 66, 67, 70
Black Sea, 41
blowhole, 10, 15–16
blubber, 12
boats, 54
botos, 47–50
bottlenose, 13, 17, 18, 36, 37,
  40
brains, 22–23
Brazil, 49–50, 87
breathing, 15–16
bycatch, 26

California, Gulf of, 57
calves, 20–22
Canada, 45, 73
*Captive Cetaceans: A
  Handbook for Campaigners*
  (Mooney), 65–66
captivity, 59–74
capture, 59–65, 66
Cetacea, 10
cetaceans, 10
chemicals, 43–50, 56–58
Chile, 41
China, 48, 82–84, 89
classification, 10–11
clicking, 16–20
"cold water cowboys," 66
communication, 16–20
communities, 20–21
Cone, Marla, 78
Cousteau, Jacques-Yves, 15,
  18

Delphinidae, 11
description. *See individual
  characteristics*
die-offs, 52–53, 55–58
diet, 14, 15
diving, 15–16
dolphin meat, 34–35
Dolphin Protection Consumer
  Information Act, 28, 77
Dolphin Research Center, 68

dolphins
  Amazon River, 48–50
  baiji, 48, 82–84
  black, 41
  botos, 47–50
  bottlenose, 13, 17, 18, 36, 37,
    40
  common, 31
  Ganges River, 44, 46–47
  Hector's, 31
  Indus River, 46–47
  pink, 47–50
  Risso's, 11, 36
  river, 11, 18
  spotted, 13, 18, 37
  striped, 37
  susu, 44, 46–47
  tucuxi, 11, 87
  white, 89
  white-sided, 31, 37, 66
  Yangtze River, 48, 82–84
"dolphin safe," 28, 77, 79
Dolphins (Cousteau), 15
"Dolphins in Crisis"
  (National Geographic), 17
Dolphins of the World
  (Wilson), 12, 13
dorsals, 10–11, 13

Eastern Tropical Pacific
  (ETP), 27–29, 75
echolocation, 16–20
endangerment, 69
  see also pollution; killing
Environmental News Network
  (ENN), 89
European Union (EU), 80, 82
Evans, Peter G. H., 34
eyes, 16

Faeroes (islands), 38–40

families, 20–21
feeding, 14–15, 18
*Field Guide to Whales and
  Dolphins in the Philippines, A*
  (Ma), 45
fins, 12
Fish Aggregating Devices
  (FADs), 79
fishing (hunting), 20, 25
flippers, 12
flukes, 12
food chain, 58
Free Willy (film), 84–85
Free Willy Foundation, 85
Frontline (TV show), 71
Futo, 37, 38

Ganges River, 44, 46–47
gill nets. *See* nets
Goldsberry, Don, 64
Gorman, Brian, 53
Greenpeace International, 49,
  80–81, 82, 89, 90
Griffin, Ted, 64
grindagrup (hunt), 38

Harbor Branch
  Oceanographic Institution,
  91
helicopters, 28
Herman, Rick, 91
Hong Kong, 89
Hoyt, Erich, 61–62
Hudson Bay, 66
hunting (fishing), 20, 25
hydrophone, 18

Iki Island, 36
"Indiscriminate Slaughter at
  Sea" (National Audubon

Society), 32
Indus Dolphin Reserve, 47
Indus River, 47
injuries, 68
Institute of Hydrobiology, 48
intelligence, 22–25
International Whaling
  Commission, 41
International Dolphin
  Conservation Program Act
  (IDCPA), 77, 79
Iqbal, Nadeem, 47

Japan, 34–38
Jari River, 50

Katsumoto, 36
Keiko, 84–87
Khalid, Umeed, 47
killer whales
  false, 37
  see also orcas
killing, 37–40

legends, 6
license plates, 91
life span, 22
Lilly, John, 24
longline, 32–33
Los Angeles Times
  (newspaper), 48, 78, 84
Low Frequency Active Sonar
  (LFA), 19
lungs, 15

Ma, Jose, 45
MacAskie, Ian, 66
Man and Dolphin (Lilly), 24
Marine Biological
  Association of the United

Kingdom, 63
Marineland, 60, 68
Marine Mammal Protection
  Act (MMPA), 24, 73–76, 87
Marine Mammals and Man
  (Wood), 69
Marine Mammal Stranding
  Center, 90
marine parks, 67–68
marine preserves. *See*
  preserves
marine sanctuaries. *See*
  sanctuaries
McBain, Jim, 71
meat. *See* dolphin meat
Mediterranean Sea, 88
Mexico, 57–58, 85
military, 19, 70–73
minkes, 10, 41
MMPA (Marine Mammal
  Protection Act), 24, 73–76,
  87
"Moby Doll," 62
monofilament, 32
Mooney, Jerye, 65, 66
muchame ("sea pig"), 40
muscles, 12
myths, 6

Namu, 64
Nanuk Enterprises, 66
narwhal, 40
National Audobon Society, 32
National Geographic
  (magazine), 17, 54
National Marine Fisheries
  Service, 33, 66, 75
National Marine Protection,
  Research and Sanctuaries
  Act, 87

National Oceanic and Atmospheric Administration (NOAA), 53, 55
National Resources Defense Council, 19
Natural History of Whales and Dolphins, The (Evans), 34
navy, 19, 70–73
"Navy Sonar System Threatens Marine Animals," 19
nets, 27–33, 35, 79-82
NOAA (National Oceanic and Atmospheric Administration), 53, 55
noises, 17–18, 24
Norris, Kenneth S., 17, 30, 35, 38
North Atlantic Treaty Organization (NATO), 19
Norway, 41
numbers, 29, 30, 37

oceanariums, 67, 68
Odontoceti, 10
oil. *See* whale oil
OrcaInfo, 68
orcas, 60–62, 64, 66, 74
  see also whales, killer
Orinoco River, 49

Pakistan, 46–47
parks, 68
Pawlyna, Andrea, 89
PCBs (polychlorinated biphenyls), 37, 45, 55–56
Perrin, William, 75
Peru, 40–41
Philippines, 46
Phocoenidae, 11

"pingers," 78
plastic, 50–52
Platanistidae, 11
pods, 18, 21
poisons, 7, 35, 37, 43, 45, 55–58
pollution, 7, 35, 43–52, 56–58, 89
porpoises
  Dall's, 31, 37, 69, 82
  harbor, 11, 18, 40
preserves, 87–90
prey, 14, 15
Protected Animal of the First Order, 82, 83
purse seine, 27–29, 64, 75–77, 79

Radio Shack, 78
red tide, 55, 56–58
respiration, 15
"running," 13–14

sanctuaries, 87–90
Sanctuary for the Protection of the Cetaceans, 88
schools, 18, 21
"sea pig," 40
search and recovery, 70
Seattle Public Aquarium, 64
Sea World, 60, 64, 69–71, 85
sensitivity, 12–13
Shamu, 60, 64
size, 11
skin, 12–13
slaughter, 37, 38–40
sleep, 23
slipstream, 21
smile, 17

sonar, 16–20
sounds, 17–18, 24
South Pacific Forum, 79, 81
speed, 13–14
statistics, 29, 30, 37
submarines, 19
susu, 44, 46–47
Suzuki, David, 60
swimmer-diversion missions, 72
swimming, 11–12

Taiji, 37, 38, 74
Tan, Lorenzo, 45
Tarawa Declaration, 79, 81
temperature, 14
Tempest, Rone, 48, 84
Three Gorges Dam, 48
tides, 55, 56–58
Tongling, 82
traits. *See* individual
  characteristics
tucuxi, 11, 87
tuna
  "dolphin-safe," 77, 79
  yellowfin, 26–33, 79
  yellowtail, 36
Turkey, 41
types, 10–11

United Nations (UN), 32,
  79–80, 82
U.S. Navy, 19, 70–73

vision, 16

Wang Ding, 48
websites, 38, 41, 47, 68, 81
Whale and Dolphin
  Conservation Society, 90
whale oil, 34
whales
  beluga, 40, 63, 66, 67, 70
  blue, 10
  false killer, 37
  humpback, 10, 89
  killer, 11, 36, 73, 84–87
  long-finned pilot, 38–40
  minke, 10, 41
  narwhal, 40
  northern right, 31
  orca, 60–62, 64, 66, 74
  pilot, 40
  short-finned pilot, 37
  sperm, 10, 34
  "toothed," 10
*Whales, Dolphins and
  Porpoises*, 63, 66–67, 69, 88
whale watching, 88
Willy, 84–85
Wilson, Ben, 12, 13, 15–18
Wilson, Keith, 89
Wood, Forrest G., 69
World Wide Fund for Nature,
  88
Würsig, Bernd, 44, 46

Yangtze River Dolphin
  Preserve, 84
yellowfin, 26–33, 79
yellowtail, 36

Picture Credits

About the Author

Stuart A. Kallen is the author of more than 150 nonfiction books for children and young adults. He has written on topics ranging from the theory of relativity to rock-and-roll history to life on the American frontier. In addition, Mr. Kallen has written award-winning children's videos and television scripts. In his spare time, Stuart A. Kallen swims with the dolphins and is a singer/songwriter/guitarist in San Diego, California.